APHRODITE'S TRADE

THE LOCHLAINN SEABROOK COLLECTION

AMERICAN CIVIL WAR
Abraham Lincoln Was a Liberal, Jefferson Davis Was a Conservative: The Missing Key to Understanding the American Civil War
Confederacy 101: Amazing Facts You Never Knew About America's Oldest Political Tradition
Confederate Blood and Treasure: An Interview With Lochlainn Seabrook
Everything You Were Taught About African-Americans and the Civil War is Wrong, Ask a Southerner!
Everything You Were Taught About the Civil War is Wrong, Ask a Southerner!
Give This Book to a Yankee! A Southern Guide to the Civil War For Northerners
Lincoln's War: The Real Cause, the Real Winner, the Real Loser
The Great Yankee Coverup: What the North Doesn't Want You to Know About Lincoln's War!
The Ultimate Civil War Quiz Book: How Much Do You Really Know About America's Most Misunderstood Conflict?
Women in Gray: A Tribute to the Ladies Who Supported the Southern Confederacy

CONFEDERATE MONUMENTS
Confederate Monuments: Why Every American Should Honor Confederate Soldiers and Their Memorials

CONFEDERATE FLAG
Confederate Flag Facts: What Every American Should Know About Dixie's Southern Cross
What the Confederate Flag Means to Me: Americans Speak Out in Defense of Southern Honor, Heritage, and History

SECESSION
All We Ask Is To Be Let Alone: The Southern Secession Fact Book

SLAVERY
Everything You Were Taught About American Slavery is Wrong, Ask a Southerner!
Slavery 101: Amazing Facts You Never Knew About America's "Peculiar Institution"

CHILDREN
Honest Jeff and Dishonest Abe: A Southern Children's Guide to the Civil War
Saddle, Sword, and Gun: A Biography of Nathan Bedford Forrest For Teens

NATHAN BEDFORD FORREST
A Rebel Born: A Defense of Nathan Bedford Forrest - Confederate General, American Legend (winner of the 2011 Jefferson Davis Historical Gold Medal)
A Rebel Born: The Screenplay (film about N. B. Forrest)
Forrest! 99 Reasons to Love Nathan Bedford Forrest
Give 'Em Hell Boys! The Complete Military Correspondence of Nathan Bedford Forrest
I Rode With Forrest! Confederate Soldiers Who Served With the World's Greatest Cavalry Leader
Nathan Bedford Forrest and African-Americans: Yankee Myth, Confederate Fact
Nathan Bedford Forrest and the Battle of Fort Pillow: Yankee Myth, Confederate Fact
Nathan Bedford Forrest and the Ku Klux Klan: Yankee Myth, Confederate Fact
Nathan Bedford Forrest: Southern Hero, American Patriot - Honoring a Confederate Icon and the Old South
Saddle, Sword, and Gun: A Biography of Nathan Bedford Forrest For Teens
The God of War: Nathan Bedford Forrest As He Was Seen By His Contemporaries
The Quotable Nathan Bedford Forrest: Selections From the Writings and Speeches of the Confederacy's Most Brilliant Cavalryman

QUOTABLE SERIES
The Alexander H. Stephens Reader: Excerpts From the Works of a Confederate Founding Father
The Quotable Alexander H. Stephens: Selections From the Writings and Speeches of the Confederacy's First Vice President
The Quotable Jefferson Davis: Selections From the Writings and Speeches of the Confederacy's First President
The Quotable Nathan Bedford Forrest: Selections From the Writings and Speeches of the Confederacy's Most Brilliant Cavalryman
The Quotable Robert E. Lee: Selections From the Writings and Speeches of the South's Most Beloved Civil War General
The Quotable Stonewall Jackson: Selections From the Writings and Speeches of the South's Most Famous General
The Unquotable Abraham Lincoln: The President's Quotes They Don't Want You To Know!

CIVIL WAR BATTLES
Encyclopedia of the Battle of Franklin - A Comprehensive Guide to the Conflict that Changed the Civil War
Nathan Bedford Forrest and the Battle of Fort Pillow: Yankee Myth, Confederate Fact
The Battle of Franklin: Recollections of Confederate and Union Soldiers
The Battle of Nashville: Recollections of Confederate and Union Soldiers
The Battle of Spring Hill: Recollections of Confederate and Union Soldiers

CONSTITUTIONAL HISTORY
The Articles of Confederation Explained: A Clause-by-Clause Study of America's First Constitution
The Constitution of the Confederate States of America Explained: A Clause-by-Clause Study of the South's Magna Carta

VICTORIAN CONFEDERATE LITERATURE
Rise Up and Call Them Blessed: Victorian Tributes to the Confederate Soldier, 1861-1901
The God of War: Nathan Bedford Forrest As He Was Seen By His Contemporaries
The Old Rebel: Robert E. Lee As He Was Seen By His Contemporaries
Victorian Confederate Poetry: The Southern Cause in Verse, 1861-1901

ABRAHAM LINCOLN
Abraham Lincoln: The Southern View - Demythologizing America's Sixteenth President
Lincolnology: The Real Abraham Lincoln Revealed in His Own Words - A Study of Lincoln's Suppressed, Misinterpreted, and Forgotten Writings and Speeches
Lincoln's War: The Real Cause, the Real Winner, the Real Loser
The Great Impersonator! 99 Reasons to Dislike Abraham Lincoln
The Unholy Crusade: Lincoln's Legacy of Destruction in the American South
The Unquotable Abraham Lincoln: The President's Quotes They Don't Want You To Know!

NATURAL HISTORY
North America's Amazing Mammals: An Encyclopedia for the Whole Family
The Concise Book of Owls: A Guide to Nature's Most Mysterious Birds
The Concise Book of Tigers: A Guide to Nature's Most Remarkable Cats

PARANORMAL
Carnton Plantation Ghost Stories: True Tales of the Unexplained from Tennessee's Most Haunted Civil War House!
UFOs and Aliens: The Complete Guidebook

FAMILY HISTORIES
The Blakeneys: An Etymological, Ethnological, and Genealogical Study - Uncovering the Mysterious Origins of the Blakeney Family and Name
The Caudills: An Etymological, Ethnological, and Genealogical Study - Exploring the Name and National Origins of a European-American Family
The McGavocks of Carnton Plantation: A Southern History - Celebrating One of Dixie's Most Noble Confederate Families and Their Tennessee Home

MIND, BODY, SPIRIT
Autobiography of a Non-Yogi: A Scientist's Journey From Hinduism to Christianity (Dr. Amitava Dasgupta, with Lochlainn Seabrook)
Britannia Rules: Goddess-Worship in Ancient Anglo-Celtic Society - An Academic Look at the United Kingdom's Matricentric Spiritual Past
Christ Is All and In All: Rediscovering Your Divine Nature and the Kingdom Within
Christmas Before Christianity: How the Birthday of the "Sun" Became the Birthday of the "Son"
Jesus and the Gospel of Q: Christ's Pre-Christian Teachings As Recorded in the New Testament
Jesus and the Law of Attraction: The Bible-Based Guide to Creating Perfect Health, Wealth, and Happiness Following Christ's Simple Formula
Seabrook's Bible Dictionary of Traditional and Mystical Christian Doctrines
The Bible and the Law of Attraction: 99 Teachings of Jesus, the Apostles, and the Prophets
The Book of Kelle: An Introduction to Goddess-Worship and the Great Celtic Mother-Goddess Kelle, Original Blessed Lady of Ireland
The Goddess Dictionary of Words and Phrases: Introducing a New Core Vocabulary for the Women's Spirituality Movement

WOMEN
Aphrodite's Trade: The Hidden History of Prostitution Unveiled
Princess Diana: Modern Day Moon-Goddess - A Psychoanalytical and Mythological Look at Diana Spencer's Life, Marriage, and Death (with Dr. Jane Goldberg)
Women in Gray: A Tribute to the Ladies Who Supported the Southern Confederacy

REPRINTS
A Short History of the Confederate States of America (author Jefferson Davis; editor Lochlainn Seabrook)

Lochlainn Seabrook does not author books for fame and fortune, but for the love of writing and sharing his knowledge.

SeaRavenPress.com

APHRODITE'S TRADE

THE HIDDEN HISTORY OF PROSTITUTION UNVEILED

LOCHLAINN SEABROOK

JEFFERSON DAVIS HISTORICAL GOLD MEDAL WINNER

FOREWORD BY XAVIERA HOLLANDER
Author of the International Bestseller *The Happy Hooker*

Diligently Researched for the Elucidation of the Reader

2020

Sea Raven Press, Nashville, Tennessee, USA

APHRODITE'S TRADE

Published by
Sea Raven Press, Cassidy Ravensdale, President
PO Box 1484, Spring Hill, Tennessee 37174-1484 USA
SeaRavenPress.com • searavenpress@gmail.com

Copyright © 1993, 1994, 1999, 2010, 2011, 2020 Lochlainn Seabrook
in accordance with U.S. and international copyright laws and regulations, as stated and protected under the Berne Union for the Protection of Literary and Artistic Property (Berne Convention), and the Universal Copyright Convention (the UCC). All rights reserved under the Pan-American and International Copyright Conventions.

1st SRP paperback edition, 1st printing, August 2010 • ISBN: 978-0-9827700-4-7
2nd SRP paperback edition, 1st printing, August 2011 • ISBN: 978-0-9838185-0-2
2nd SRP paperback edition, 2nd printing, October 2020 • ISBN: 978-0-9838185-0-2
1st SRP hardcover edition, 1st printing, October 2020 • ISBN: 978-1-943737-89-5

ISBN: 978-0-9838185-0-2 (paperback)
Library of Congress Control Number: 2011934617

This work is the copyrighted intellectual property of Lochlainn Seabrook and has been registered with the Copyright Office at the Library of Congress in Washington, D.C., USA. No part of this work (including text, covers, drawings, photos, illustrations, maps, images, diagrams, etc.), in whole or in part, may be used, reproduced, stored in a retrieval system, or transmitted, in any form or by any means now known or hereafter invented, without written permission from the publisher. The sale, duplication, hire, lending, copying, digitalization, or reproduction of this material, in any manner or form whatsoever, is also prohibited, and is a violation of federal, civil, and digital copyright law, which provides severe civil and criminal penalties for any violations.

Aphrodite's Trade: The Hidden History of Prostitution Unveiled, by Lochlainn Seabrook. Foreword by Xaviera Hollander. Includes bibliographical references and an index.

Front and back cover design and art, book design, layout, and interior art by Lochlainn Seabrook
All images, graphic design, graphic art, and illustrations copyright © Lochlainn Seabrook
All images selected, placed, manipulated, and/or created by Lochlainn Seabrook
Cover images and design copyright © Lochlainn Seabrook

The views expressed in this book are those of the publisher.

DEDICATION

To Aphrodite and Flora

Aphrodite is the Greek Love-Goddess who ruled sacred prostitution in ancient Corinth, and who was known as *Porne* (the "Harlot").

Flora is the Roman Spring-Goddess, also known as *Meretrix* (the "Whore"). For 2,500 years she has been the Special Deity, Matron, and Protector of Prostitutes. Until the 3rd Century Flora was venerated at her own special May Day festival, the *Floralia*, which lasted from April 28 to May 3, in orgiastic rites, public body worship and licentious dancing.

EPIGRAPH

I tell you truthfully that . . . prostitutes will enter the Kingdom of God before most of those who call themselves "Christians" (Matthew 21:31).

JESUS
descendant of a long line of prostitutes, including
Thamar, Rachab, Ruth, and Bathseheba

CONTENTS

Ancient Whore Wisdom From the Great Whore-Mother-Goddess Herself - 13
Notes To the Reader - 17
Foreword, by Xaviera Hollander - 21
Acknowledgments - 25
Introduction, by Lochlainn Seabrook - 27

Chapter 1
THE PREHISTORIC ORIGINS OF PROSTITUTION
The Oldest Profession - 31
From Promiscuity to Pair-Bonding - 31
The Human Sexual Condition: Programmed for Polygamy - 32
Our Enlarging Brain & Immature Babies - 32
Of Sisterhoods & Brotherhoods - 33

Chapter 2
CONTRACTUAL SEX
Food for Sex, Sex for Food - 35
The Prostitution Gene - 35
Men as Providing Objects, Women as Sex Objects - 36
Mother Nature, the Sexist - 37
Our Laws Reflect Our Prostitutionary Inheritance - 38
Defining the Words "Marriage" & "Wife" - 38
Of Whores & Wives: Havelock Ellis on Marriage - 39
The Unfair Demonization of Prostitutes - 39

Chapter 3
THE SACRED PRIESTESS
The Bearers of Shakti - 40
Origins of the Word Whore - 40
Ancient Whores of Myth & Legend - 40
Mari: The Great Triple-Goddess & Divine Whore-Mother - 41

Functions of the Ancient Prostitute - 42
Sacrality of the Number Thirteen - 43

Chapter 4
EVOLUTION OF THE HOLY HARLOT
The Whore as Virgin-Mother - 44
The Sin of Monogamy - 44
Women on Top: Ancient Relationships - 45
Lesbians, Spiritual Sisters, & All-Female Communities - 45
The Enduring Female Relationship - 46

Chapter 5
WHEN JUDAISM WAS MATRIARCHAL
Goddess-Worship Among the Israelites - 47
Jewish Whore Wisdom - 47
Jewish Serpent Cults - 48
Prostitution at the Jewish Temple - 48
The Many Names of the Jewish Whore-Goddess - 49
Palestine, the Hora Dance, & the Jewish Lunar Calender - 49
Jewish Women Who Tried to Revive Goddess-Worship - 50
The Semitic Goddess Hor & the Vulva-Worshiping Horites - 50
The Creation of the Whore of Babylon - 51
Destruction of the Matriarchate by Patriarchal Judaism - 51

Chapter 6
ARCHETYPES, FATHERS, & POLYGAMY
The Invincible Whore-Mother - 53
Men Generally Make Poor Husbands & Fathers - 53
Coercing Men Into Monogamous Marriage - 54
Women Are Naturally Polygamous - 54

Chapter 7
MARY & THE CHRISTIAN PATRIARCHAL TAKEOVER
The Paganization of Mary & Jesus - 56
Goddess' Christing Ritual - 57
Christianization of the Triple-Goddess - 57
Mary Magdalene & the Whore Wisdom - 58
Jesus & Mary Magdalene: The Royal Bloodline - 59

How da Vinci Preserved the Divine Feminine - 60
God Began as Goddess - 61
Goddess-Worship in the Old Testament - 61
The Golden Age of Women: No Trace of God - 62
The Patriarchal Takeover: From Earth-Mother to Sky-Father - 63

Chapter 8
CHRISTIANITY'S SACRED WHORES
How the Changing Names of God Reveal His Whore-Goddess Roots - 64
Why God Was First Called El Shaddai - 65
The Whore-Goddess as Christian Saint - 65
Minne, the Cult of Mary, & the Christian Whorehouse - 66
Christianity Once Supported Prostitution - 66
The U.S. Army Legalizes Prostitution - 67

Chapter 9
COMMERCIAL PROSTITUTION & MODERN MARRIAGE
The Creation of Secular Prostitution - 69
Modern Christian Worship of the Great Whore - 69
The True Origins & Meaning of Marriage - 71
Goddess' Sacred Day - 72
The Names of God & Christ - 72
The Whore-Mother as Sun-Goddess - 73
How the Pagan Sun-Goddess Became the Christian Sun-God - 74
Christmas & the Whore-Goddess - 75
The Patriarchalization Process - 75

Chapter 10
PROSTITUTION: THE NOBLE HERITAGE
Patriarchal Marriage is Sanctioned Prostitution - 77
Horology & the Sex Worker Profession - 77
The Whore-Mother's Connection to Time, Intelligence, Life, Women, & Earth - 78
Prostitution & the Survival of *Homo Sapiens* - 78
The Light of Knowledge - 79
Aphrodite's Daughters - 79
Nurses of the Body & Soul - 80
The Women of Aphrodite's Trade - 80

APPENDICES

Appendix A: Myths About Decriminalizing Prostitution - 83
Appendix B: Positive & Negative Synonyms Used for the Word Prostitute - 89
Appendix C: Words & Phrases Used For the Profession or Act of Prostitution - 91
Appendix D: Words & Phrases Used For a House of Prostitution - 92
Appendix E: Words Used in the Past in Relationship to the Word Prostitute - 93
Appendix F: Words Used Today in Relationship to the Word Prostitute - 95
Appendix G: World Charter for Prostitutes' Rights - 97
    Laws - 97
    Human Rights - 97
    Working Conditions - 98
    Health - 98
    Services - 98
    Taxes - 98
    Public Opinion - 99
    Organization - 99
Appendix H: Human Taxonomy - 100

Bibliography - 103
Index - 125
The Author's Genealogy - 167
Meet the Author - 168
Learn More - 169

ANCIENT WHORE WISDOM
from the
GREAT WHORE-MOTHER-GODDESS HERSELF

Excerpted from the 1st-Century anonymous Gnostic Christian text:
The Thunder: Perfect Mind

I was sent forth from the power, and I have come to those who reflect upon me, and I have been found among those who seek after me.

Look upon me, you who reflect upon me, and you hearers, hear me.

You who are waiting for me, take me to yourselves.
And do not banish me from your sight.
And do not make your voice hate me, nor your hearing.

Do not be ignorant of me anywhere or at any time.
Be on your guard! Do not be ignorant of me.

For I am the first and the last, I am the honored one and the scorned one, I am the whore and the holy one, I am the wife and the virgin. I am the mother and the daughter . . . I am she whose wedding is great, and I have not taken a husband. . . .

Why do you who hate me, do you love me and hate those who love me?

You who deny me, confess me, and you who confess me, deny me.

You who tell the truth about me, lie about me, and you who have lied about me, tell the truth about me.

You who know me, be ignorant of me, and those who have not known me, let them know me.

For I am knowledge and ignorance, I am shame and boldness, I am shameless; I am ashamed.

I am strength and I am fear. I am war and peace.

Give heed to me. I am the one who is disgraced and the great one. . . .

Come forward to me, you who know me. Come forward to childhood. . . .

I am the one who has been hated everywhere and who has been loved everywhere.

I am the one whom they call Life, and you have called Death.

I am the one they call Law, and you have called Lawlessness.

I am the one whom you have pursued, and I am the one whom you have seized.

I am the one you have scattered, and you have gathered me together.

I am the one before whom you have been ashamed, and you have been shameless to me. . . .

I am the one whom you have reflected upon, and you have scorned me.

I am unlearned, and they learn from me.

I am the one whom you have despised, and you reflect upon me.

I am the one you have hidden from, and you appear to me.
But whenever you hide yourselves, I myself will appear.
And whenever you appear, I myself will hide from you. . . .

Why do you curse me and honor me?
You have wounded and you have had mercy.

Do not separate me from the first ones whom you have known.

And do not cast anyone out nor turn anyone away. . . .

I am the knowledge of my inquiry, and the finding of those who seek after me . . . of the angels who have been sent at my word, and of deities in their seasons by my counsel, and of spirits of every man who exists with me, and of women who dwell within me. . . .

I am the union and the dissolution. . . .
I am the judgment and the acquittal.
I am sinless, and the root of sin derives from me.
I am lust in outward appearance, and interior self-control exists within me. . . .

Hear me in gentleness, and learn of me in roughness. . . .
I am the one who is called Truth and Iniquity. . . .

Hear me, you hearers, and learn of my words, you who know me. . . . For I am the One who alone exists, and I have no one who will judge me.

Many are the pleasant forms which exist in . . . fleeting pleasures, which men embrace until they become sober and go up to their resting-place.

And they will find me there, and they will live, and they will not die again.

16 ～ APHRODITE'S TRADE

NOTES TO THE READER

▼ Biblical quotes and references are from the King James Version (KJV).

▼ For reasons which will be obvious, this book is specifically about, and solely dedicated to, *female* prostitution.

▼ There are many types of marriage in the world today. However, unless indicated, throughout this book when I use the word marriage I am speaking specifically of patriarchal marriage, still the norm in Western society.[1] Patriarchal marriage is defined here as a legal union in which the man is the head of the family unit, children take the father's name (patronymicism),[2] and the couple's relationship is based sex.[3] This is to be contrasted with matriarchal marriage, a legal union in which the woman is the head of the family unit, children take the mother's name (matronymicism),[4] and the couple's relationship is based on love.[5]

▼ My book *Aphrodite's Trade* deals with the weighty subject of human relationships and, just as importantly, their natural association with religion and politics. As a scientific work, I present these elements of human society as being largely predetermined by sociobiological forces. That is, they flow out of neural programming hardwired into our brains over many millions of years of primate evolution.

Contrary to the information I provide on the following pages, however, I am not a genetic determinist. I do not believe that humans are powerless to control these built-in behaviors. Quite the opposite.

While I conclude, for example, that modern marriage is built on a

---

1. While we are fast approaching a state of gylanic marriage, I assert that here in the West marriage is still largely patriarchal since it continues to favor the male in a number of respects (see below). Note: by gylany I mean a social organization (in this case, marriage) in which the woman and the man are equal, and in which there is no hierarchy. (The *gy* element in gylany derives from the Greek word for woman, *gyne*, and the *an* element derives from the Greek word for man, *andros*.)
2. Patronymicism is also known as patronymy: naming after the father, by the father, or through the father's family.
3. This is not to say that all patriarchal marriages are based on sex and not love. Only that this is true as a general biological rule.
4. Matronymicism is also known as metronymy: naming after the mother, by the mother, or through the mother's family.
5. This is not to say that all matriarchal marriages are based on love and not sex. Only that this is true as a general biological rule.

prehistoric prostitutionary relationship between men and women and that we are naturally polygamous beings, at the same time I maintain that we possess the mental capacity to override these programmings if we so desire.

It is true that the vast majority of humans are promiscuous and even polygamous to one extent or another, even in the highly monogamous West, where infidelity and divorce rates are far above 50 percent. Yes, we are driven to these things by biological instinct. But it is my personal belief that this does not also mean that these types of behaviors are uncontrollable.

Rational thinking is one of the hallmarks of the human animal, as is spiritual belief. In the West, when Nature (the drive toward polygamy) and Society (the drive toward monogamy) diverge at the fork in the road of life, it is up to the individual to choose his or her path.

The path of Nature is easiest—because we are hardwired for it. Yet, in a monogamous society such as ours it often causes the most pain and suffering to all those involved, even to the unmarried.

Simultaneously, the path of Society is more difficult—because it goes against are innate programming. Despite this, while it may thwart our biological impulses, it offers rich rewards because it fulfills our intense need for social conformity (a survival instinct). For in a monogamously oriented culture like ours, monogamy tends to bring stability, longevity, and ultimately happiness, or at least contentment, to the adult human relationship.

It is for these reasons that, despite the scientific findings and the words that follow, I am pro-monogamy, pro-marriage, pro-fidelity, and pro-family. Saint Paul said it better than anyone: "It is better to marry than to burn."[6] And he is correct, for numerous studies show that, on average, married people are healthier, happier, live longer, are more trusted, admired, and respected, make more money, and even get more promotions, than the unmarried. In our society it is a disadvantage to be either single or polygamous.

But being a political and religious conservative (libertarian) does not mean that I am also a social conservative who condemns prostitution. To the contrary, like Saint Augustine, William F. Buckley, Jr., John Stossel, Governor Jesse Ventura, and many other conservatives and libertarians, I see the sex care provider industry, and in particular prostitution, as an

---

6. 1 Corinthians 7:9. What Saint Paul meant by "burn" has many possible interpretations. I take it to mean simply "to suffer" the mostly negative social, psychological, physical, emotional, sexual, financial, and occupational consequences of being single.

indispensable safety valve for Western society, one that should be decriminalized immediately.

For me, these concepts are not mutually exclusive. Rather they are mutually inclusive, for contrary to what many of my conservative colleagues believe, no two ideas are more compatible than political libertarianism and social liberalism.

Thus, even as a conservative Christian I can say that it is not the government's job to regulate sexual behavior. Rather it is the government's job to leave the people alone. Prostitution, therefore, should be permitted, and consenting adults should be allowed to make their own decisions regarding relationships *and* morality.

The path we each choose, toward Nature or toward Society, is a personal and private one; one that should be recognized as such by the State. As long as the choice we make concerning "affairs of the heart" does not violate the constitutional rights of anyone else, who we choose to associate ourselves with on an intimate level should be left to the individual. For as my libertarian cousin Thomas Jefferson once wisely observed, the people are the best protectors of their own rights.

L.S.

20 ~ APHRODITE'S TRADE

FOREWORD

by Xaviera Hollander
Author of the international bestseller *The Happy Hooker*

I'M delighted to write the foreword to this wonderfully captivating book. In *Aphrodite's Trade*, the author, popular historian Lochlainn Seabrook, takes us on a fascinating journey of discovery in order to unveil the long suppressed origins and development of prostitution.

In this scientific but humane exploration, we learn that the modern sex work industry has its roots in the prostitutionary relationships of our prehistoric ancestors. Long before there was such a thing as monogamy, early women—who lived with their children and other females in all-women groups called "matriarchies"—found it advantageous to offer men sex in exchange for food and protection. Thus the most sexual females garnered the most nutrients and lived the longest, passing their DNA on into the gene pool. At the same time, the males who provided the most material comfort were able to mate with the most females, making their DNA the most successful.

We today, every woman and every man, are the result of this phenomenon, commonly known to anthropologists as "contractual sex." What this means, in short, is that prostitution is part of our evolutionary heritage, and that trading sex for money is as instinctual to humans as eating and breathing. We are genetically hardwired for prostitution, "Aphrodite's Trade," as Mr. Seabrook very appropriately calls it. Indeed, this is why in ancient times prostitution became an integral part of nearly every religion on earth, including Judaism. At one point, realizing that suppressing it did more damage to monogamous marriage than allowing it, even Christianity adopted prostitution.

One of the many things I love about this book is that it teaches without prejudice, without malice, without cattiness. Written in a straight-forward manner and with true integrity, its deep insights into human nature make it easy to relate to. On a more personal level, it was liberating for me to learn that my former profession as "the Happy Hooker" was not a crime in the eyes of Nature. I was merely following the honorable, and often sacred, path of millions of women before me, from prehistoric times to the present.

Based on logic and compassion, Mr. Seabrook discusses the many common sense reasons why prostitution should be decriminalized. His arguments will challenge even the most vociferous critics of the sex work industry.

This is the first book I've ever read that provides a holistic history of prostitution, from its beginnings as a survival mechanism in the mists of prehistory to its culmination in the 21st Century as a commercialized business. A daring work, the author even takes on radical feminists, who wrongheadedly continue to preach that "biology is not destiny." "Biology is most assuredly destiny," Mr. Seabrook insists, backing up his assertion with numerous academic studies from various scientific fields.

The author's approach is evenhanded: while this book is pro-female, it's not anti-male. While it's pro-prostitution, it's not anti-religious. While it's provocative, it's not anti-tradition. Indeed, Mr. Seabrook, a conservative Christian, sees himself as following in the footsteps of others from this group who favored decriminalizing prostitution; namely Saint Augustine and the founder of *The National Review*, William F. Buckley, Jr.

In the final analysis, *Aphrodite's Trade* is an important book with much to teach us. For this soulful work is based not only on hard facts and intellectual reasoning, but on a heartfelt sympathy for the human condition as well: if one prostitute suffers, all of society suffers.

To me the most vital aspect of Mr. Seabrook's book is that by revealing the truth about the origins and evolution of prostitution, it liberates and empowers all the working girls out there. This is a big step forward for a profession that's gotten an unfair rap for far too long.

And there's an important message for men here, as well. Whether you're a doctor or a lawyer, a plumber or a police officer, you will always need the "feminine touch" that only the companionship of a woman can satisfy. Sex workers fulfill this need honestly, efficiently, and with a minimum of drama and complications. As long as you need us, we will be there for you. Since our needs are mutually agreeable *and* based firmly in biology, it is obvious that prostitution will exist in one form or another until the end of time. Making it a crime is thus foolish and counterproductive to society.

To all you working girls, and to all those contemplating a career in the sex care providing business, let us take the power, majesty, and honor inherent in our profession and fully embrace it. For as *Aphrodite's Trade* shows, we are not tramps and sluts, we are not outlaws and felons. We are divine in the truest sense of the word. We are powerful goddesses in our own right, the very offspring of Aphrodite herself.

Love,
Xaviera Hollander
August 2010
Amsterdam, Holland
www.xavierahollander.com

24 ~ APHRODITE'S TRADE

ACKNOWLEDGMENTS

Special thanks to my wife Cassidy, my daughters Dixie and Fiona, and to Margo St. James, Norma Jean Almodovar, and Gail Pheterson, for their assistance, enthusiasm, and charitableness during the writing of this book. Gratitude also to the One.

26 ~ APHRODITE'S TRADE

INTRODUCTION

THIS book has been written with the greatest respect for all religions and for all beliefs. In fact, I consider *Aphrodite's Trade* to be not only a scientific work, but a religious (thealogical) one as well. But where, some might ask, is the connection between religion and prostitution?

As I will show in the following pages, prostitution has long been regarded as a sacred profession, one integrally associated with religion. It is only in recent times that it has become debased, criminalized, demonized, commercialized, and cut off from its religious roots.

It is my hope that this book will renew some of the beauty and esteem formerly accorded prostitution, which I consider the world's most prestigious, and honest, profession.

The work you now hold in your hand has already saved one life. Maybe it will save others.

Lochlainn Seabrook
Nashville, Tennessee
Summer 2010

APHRODITE'S TRADE

1
THE PREHISTORIC ORIGINS OF PROSTITUTION

THE OLDEST PROFESSION

CONTRARY to conventional "wisdom," prostitution, or what I call Aphrodite's Trade, has a long and noble legacy, one that began hundreds of thousands of years ago among our prehistoric ancestors. This indeed makes it not only the world's oldest profession, but, as we will see, the profession on which both monogamous marriage and human society were originally founded.

FROM PROMISCUITY TO PAIR-BONDING

At one time early humans were promiscuous. Like our closest living relatives, the gorilla, chimpanzee, and orangutan, they were pansexual; that is, prehistoric women and men engaged in sexual activities with all other group members, female and male, young and old.

This sexual behavioral pattern would eventually change, however, from rampant promiscuity to one in which we formed pair-bonds based around female prostitution.

This transformation occurred around 1 million years ago in an early human ancestor known as *Homo erectus*. Any behavior that spans such an enormous length of time will become biologically programmed into that animal's genetic code. And this is precisely what happened in humans when we switched from promiscuity to pair-bonding.

To this day, because it is now a genetically determined behavior, pair-bonding is the type of bonding that the majority of women and men in every culture and society engage most actively in. What is the name of this pair-bond?

THE HUMAN SEXUAL CONDITION: PROGRAMMED FOR POLYGAMY

There are some individuals who would call it "lifetime monogamy." But they would be wrong. In fact, anthropological studies show that humans are not designed for lifetime monogamy, and that even in societies (such as the U.S. and the U.K.) where lifetime monogamy is held to be the ideal, only a tiny fraction of couples actually practice it.[7]

To the contrary, nearly all people, following our prehistoric ancestor's basic mating pattern, form a *temporary* pair-bond with a single mate, separate, then go in search of a new partner with whom she or he forms another brief, tenuous bond. This primal custom, known as a "consort bond," is overtly reflected in our obsession with romance and dating, and in our extremely high rates of out-of-wedlock births, children with multiple partners, desertion, infidelity, divorce, and remarriage.

Some go even further by incorrectly referring to this type of short-term intimate bonding as "serial monogamy." An objective observer will quickly realize, however, that our love of short-term pair-bonding is actually a form of what would be more accurately called "serial polygamy": having a series of temporary monogamous relationships; not simultaneously (as in traditional polygamy), but in succession, spread out over time.

More to the point, the modern human practice of both serial polygamy, *and* the far less popular lifetime monogamy, are rooted firmly in the soil of prostitution, an element without which no sexual relationship could exist.

Let us look now at the evolutionary background of our prostitution-based sexual behavior.

OUR ENLARGING BRAIN & IMMATURE BABIES

With the passage of time, various biological pressures caused the prehistoric human brain to increase in size (a process well-documented in the human fossil record). This began no doubt when early humans went from independent foraging-and-scavenging groups (like other living nonhuman apes), to cooperative hunting-and-gathering communities, a more complex lifestyle requiring more brain power.

Whatever the precise origins of this phenomenon, with the heads of human infants now larger in size, they had to be born sooner in order to fit

---

7. By "lifelong monogamy" I mean bonding (that is, dating, marrying, and having sex) with only one individual during one's entire lifetime.

through the birth canal. This meant, in turn, that our species' babies were gradually born in a state of greater and greater immaturity.

In comparison to humans, other primate babies remain (and develop) in the womb for a longer period of time, and so mature rather quickly after they are born. This means that they require only a moderate amount of parental care.

After our brains began to enlarge, however, human infants were gradually born more and more "prematurely." Not yet, fully developed, they now needed *more*, not less, parental care.

OF SISTERHOODS & BROTHERHOODS
Up until this time, human mothers—like nearly all other living primate mothers continue to do—raised their offspring by themselves, in great all-female groups called "sisterhoods," or "matriarchies." As such, a mother and her children were the original nuclear family, which is why the earliest artistic portrayals of family life were of a mother and child, with no father present.[8]

Indeed, among most of the roughly 635 species of living primates, fatherhood and the two-parent family unit are literally all but unknown. Most primate males live apart from the sisterhoods as what primatologists call "vagabonds," in all-male groups or hunting parties known as "brotherhoods," "patriarchies," or "bachelorhoods."[9]

---

8. Knowledge of the "mother and child" relationship as the true nuclear family lasted well into the historic period. One has only to think of the ancient Egyptian drawings of the Virgin Mother Isis nursing her Savior Son Horus. These portrayals were later copied by the early Christian Church and appended to the figure of the Virgin Mary. Pictures of Mary nursing (or holding) her infant Savior Son Jesus are still among the most common and most popular images in Christian art and iconography. Note the complete absence of a father-figure in these particular representations.

9. Why did early humans naturally divide themselves into female and male groups, live separately, and know nothing of monogamy and the two-parent family? Biology, of course. Evidence for this comes from our physical bodies, in what is called sexual dimorphism: it is an observable fact that the average human male has larger, thicker bones than a human female, that he has a larger skull (with a prominent brow ridge), larger muscles, and a larger heart and lungs. He is also taller and generally more robust from head to toe. Why? Because Nature originally designed men for the dangerous and physically demanding task of hunting big-game. The average woman, on the other hand, has smaller, thinner bones, a smaller skull (with no brow ridge), smaller muscles, and a smaller heart and lungs. She also possesses wide flaring hips, is shorter and more gracile from head to toe, her eyes are bigger, and her hair and skin are softer than a man's. Why? Because Nature originally designed her for the very different occupations of child rearing and food gathering. These facts alone prove that "biology is destiny," contrary to what some, radical feminists in particular, preach. The separate sisterhoods and brotherhoods of our early male and female ancestors reflect this truth perfectly. Even though we in the West no longer segregate ourselves by gender (which is lamentable in some cases; studies consistently reveal, for example, that children who attend single-gender schools are almost always happier and produce higher test scores than children from coed institutions), we still retain Nature's original sexually dimorphic body designs, a vestige of the very period in which prostitutionary relationships

And so it always was for the human primate as well,[10] who thus never evolved an instinct for fatherhood (since prehistoric females were the only ones who parented). That is, until the change from small-brained mature infants to large-brained immature infants. Now the burden of child rearing was so great that females needed extra help in order to protect and feed their young. It is out of this simple need that we find the origins of prostitution.

---

first arose among our species.
10. For those who have forgotten, or who are not aware of, *Homo sapiens'* place on the tree of life, please refer to my taxonomic chart in Appendix H.

2
CONTRACTUAL SEX

FOOD FOR SEX, SEX FOR FOOD

LOOKING around them, our female primate ancestors found a large untapped work force in the nomadic bachelorhood groups of vagabond males. The question was how to entice these independent creatures into giving up their wandering lifestyle in order to serve the interests and needs (sustenance and security) of the females.

The answer was not long in coming: the females would enlist the aid of the footloose males by offering them sex in exchange for food and protection. This arrangement, well-known to anthropologists as "contractual sex," was, of course, eagerly participated in by the males. The more sex women were willing to provide, the more food and protection they received from obliging men.

Those females who prostituted themselves the most ardently lived the longest and produced the most offspring. Thus, their particular genes were passed on to the next generation in higher concentrations than those of less "sexy" or less "whorish" females.

The same process occurred among the men: those males who were most attracted to these early female prostitutes transmitted the highest amounts of DNA into the gene pool.

THE PROSTITUTION GENE

We modern humans are the product of these relationships, and so carry within us what I call the "prostitution gene." Exchanging sex for money is literally in our DNA.[11]

---

11. The term "prostitution gene" is metaphoric. It is my shorthand way of saying that our tendency to engage in prostitutionary-like relationships is an innate behavior, a survival mechanism; one that has been sculpted by evolution over hundreds of thousands of years. Whether there is an actual gene, or genes, for this behavior is something for geneticists to decide. What we can say with the utmost assuredness, however, is that we are biologically predisposed for relationships that are rooted in prostitution.

The prostitutionary relationship is not unique to the human primate. Indeed, it is a common genetically hard-wired mating strategy that is common to most primate species.

One of the more obvious examples to be found among living nonhuman primates is the chimpanzee, and in particular the species known as the Bonobo (*Pan paniscus*). For decades primatologists have noted that Bonobo males tend to share more food with sexually receptive Bonobo females than they do with less sexually receptive ones.

Revealingly though, our society does not refer to female Bonobos as "whores," "sluts," "tramps," or "trollops." Rather, such words are reserved—primarily by the uninformed and intolerant of our species—for those human sisters who, like their chimpanzee counterparts, also accept material comforts from males in exchange for sex.

As we shall see, however, a monogamously married wife is often more likely to function as a prostitute than a prostitute herself.

This is not by choice. She, like her husband, carries the prostitution gene.

MEN AS PROVIDING OBJECTS, WOMEN AS SEX OBJECTS

The result today, after at least 1 million years of this type of relationship between human females and males, is that modern women are genetically programmed to view men as providers of material support ("sugar daddies"), while modern men are genetically programmed to look at women as providers of physical pleasure ("sex objects").

To put it another way: the manner in which women and men view each other is built into our genetic code, for the very nature of all intimate relationships between women and men is inherently prehistoric and prostitutional. Thus many women continue to intentionally seek wealthy men to marry (for security), while many men continue to seek beautiful young women to marry (for sexual pleasure).

The prostitution gene manifests in other ways as well: students who offer sex to their teachers for better grades, and teachers who offer better grades for sex; female employees who offer sex to their bosses for a promotion, and bosses who offer a promotion for sex. Money may not exchange hands in these types of cases, but, according to the biological definition of Aphrodite's Trade, such acts still fall under the heading of prostitution.

While the statement that women are biologically programmed to be providers of physical pleasure just as men are biologically programmed to be providers of material support, is certainly a politically incorrect statement, Nature is not concerned with such things. Hence, in any honest discussion of this topic we ourselves must ignore the entire concept of political correctness if we are to learn and understand the facts, for political correctness nearly always hides or even suppresses the truth.

MOTHER NATURE, THE SEXIST
If the above statement is not a politically incorrect one, some may counter, then it is certainly a sexist one.

Not true. It is a scientifically accurate statement of biology, one that is born out by the fossil record and by objective studies of both living archaic *and* modern humans, and also of nonhuman primates.

Thus it is that sometimes Nature herself is a "sexist." More to the point, she is the original sexist. Why?

Like her prehistoric ancestors, the average contemporary woman unconsciously provides her man with sex in exchange for material goods (the female who controls her male partner by threatening to withhold sex is a common theme in the literary, film, and theatrical worlds), while the average contemporary man unconsciously provides his woman with material goods in exchange for sex (the sugar daddy is a popular figure as well). Sometimes this trade between partners is not as unconscious as many would like to believe.

Naturally, this biological fact has been concealed beneath the modern veneer of what we call "romance," for few are willing to admit that prostitution lies at the root of their most important relationship.

However, we have proof that it exists nonetheless: very few wives and very few husbands would choose to stay in a marriage that was asexual. For it is the security and pleasure sex brings to both females and males that forms the bedrock of the typical marital relationship, as marriage and relationship counselors continually remind us.[12]

---

12. There are, of course, exceptions to this rule, such as those (usually religious) individuals who intentionally choose a celibate partnership, or "spiritual marriage," as it is also called. These married couples have transcended the need for sex, having replaced it with genuine friendship, or what has been called Platonic love (soul love). Spiritual marriage was far more prevalent during the early centuries of the Christian Church than it is today. As Jesus taught that there is no marriage (and thus no sex) in Heaven (Matthew 22:30), ancient Christians used spiritual marriage here on earth as preparation for life in the Afterworld. For those who are suited to it, celibate marriage offers numerous benefits, as I discuss in my book *Mothers and Bachelors*.

OUR LAWS REFLECT OUR PROSTITUTIONARY INHERITANCE

So strong is our genetic programming for prostitutionary partnerships that it has even been made the foundation of modern monogamous marriage, both biblically[13] and civilly: in all fifty American States, by law, husbands are required to financially support their wives and children, while wives are legally required to provide sex to their husbands. (Those who doubt these laws are free to test them at their own risk.)

Note: while the former law remains enforceable, the latter law is decreasing in strength and popularity due to efforts by feminists. Nonetheless, it remains the law, which is why many men are still able to divorce their wives for no other reason than that their wives "did not fulfill their marital (that is sexual) obligations."

This is also why it is so difficult to convict a husband of raping his wife: until quite recently the idea of "marital rape" was unknown, and even unthinkable.

DEFINING THE WORDS "MARRIAGE" & "WIFE"

We can now plainly see that the monogamous bond between women and men began as a sexual contract based on mundane economic considerations rooted in prostitution.

As such, many see little difference between the role a wife plays and the role a prostitute plays. Feminist scholar Dr. Dale Spender, for example, defines marriage as a form of "legalized prostitution," as did Irish playwright and political activist George Bernard Shaw (1856-1950). In other words, Spender and Shaw are saying, marriage often involves "the exchange of sexual services for material support," a view that is supported by overwhelming evidence.

However (perhaps based on a knowledge of the state laws referred to above), some radical feminists take a less charitable view. Andre Dworkin, for instance, calls (patriarchal) marriage a "legal contract which sanctions rape."

Some, using the new politically correct vocabulary, now actually define a wife as "an *unpaid* sex worker," who is to be contrasted with a prostitute, who they define as "a *paid* sex worker."

---

13. See for example, Colossians 3:18.

OF WHORES & WIVES: HAVELOCK ELLIS ON MARRIAGE

The forward-thinking 19th-Century English sexologist Havelock Ellis described the difference between a wife and a prostitute this way:

> The wife who marries for money, compared with a prostitute, is the true scab [i.e., one who works for less than union wages]. She is paid less, gives much more in return in labor and care, and is absolutely bound to her master. The prostitute [on the other hand] never signs away the right over her own person, she retains her freedom and personal rights, nor is she always compelled to submit to man's embraces.

THE UNFAIR DEMONIZATION OF PROSTITUTES

Despite Ellis' enlightened view, and our biologically-determined proclivity for indulging in prostitutionary relationships, the modern prostitute, or sex worker, continues to live under an oppressive shadow of misogynistic mythology; demonized by most of her sisters, and even by many of the men (for example, police officers) who pay for her services.

Some of this is the result, of course, of ignorance.

There is no longer any excuse for such naivete, however. For the facts not only completely contradict the traditionally biased views toward prostitution, they reveal that whores (and we are using this word here in the most positive sense) functioned for thousands of years in roles of great prestige, power, and privilege.

3
THE SACRED PRIESTESS

THE BEARERS OF SHAKTI

INDEED, by the time of the Neolithic Era (about 8,000 years ago), prostitution was an integral aspect of both society and religion. Prostitutes themselves were regarded as divine bearers of the all-sacred life-bearing Feminine Power, or "Shakti."

How then did prostitutes go from being venerated in ancient times as Holy Priestesses—even as veritable deities in some cases—to their current status as "wretched sinners" and "home wreckers"?

To answer this question, let us begin by looking at the etymological background of the word "whore."

ORIGINS OF THE WORD "WHORE"

The word whore is an English corruption of the Old Semitic word *hor*, meaning "hole," "cave," or "pit." Hor, in turn, is a derivation of the pre-Judaic, Indo-European word *hora*, meaning "hour."

In fact, our modern English word hour derives from *hora*. In ancient Greece, for instance, prostitutes were called *Horae*; in Persia, *Houri*; in Babylon, *Harines*; and in Israel, *Hors*.

Now let us examine the connection between "hour" and "whore."

ANCIENT WHORES OF MYTH & LEGEND

Ancient cultures and civilizations practiced commercial and sacred prostitution, both necessary to the functioning and stability of patriarchal marriage (that is, heterosexual monogamy, comprising a father and mother, headed by the male) and of society itself.

Thus in ancient Egypt whores were known as the "Ladies of the Hour," and in present day India, where prostitute-priestesses still dispense the grace of Goddess in Hindu temples, they are called "Devadasis."

Early myths are rife with examples of the vital roles that whores once played in all human cultures. In Hindu mythology sacred prostitutes appear as the famed "Apsaras"; in Persian myth they are the celebrated "Peris"; and in Greek mythology they are known as the "Charites" or "Horae."

In Roman myth they are referred to as the "Charis," or Three "Graces," a personification of the Great Triple-Goddess (known in the region as Mari-Anna-Ishtar), whose sacred sign was the inverted three-pointed star (▽), a symbol of Goddess' magic pubic triangle, out of which her procreative powers flow.

MARI: THE GREAT TRIPLE-GODDESS & DIVINE WHORE-MOTHER
The Triple-Goddess herself is a triplicate-symbol of 1) life, 2) death, and 3) resurrection. Why?

According to the 10,000 year-old universal Moon-Mother-Goddess Creation myth, each year, during the Pagan Spring Festival or vernal equinox (appropriated by Christianity and now called "Easter" after the Anglo-Saxon Spring-Goddess Eostre), Goddess ritually kills her Divine Son, the Sun-God, the "Savior and Redeemer of the World." Who is this deity?

Among thousands of names that could be given, the sacrificial Sun-God was variously known by Pagans, Jews, and early *authentic* Christians (that is, the Gnostics) across the ancient world as Isua, Horus, Attis, Hesus, Jesus,[14] Adonis, Criti, Chrishna, Christ, Odin, and Tammuz (the tenth month of the Jewish year is still called Tammuz, a vestige from the time when the early Hebrews venerated this archetypal Pagan Savior-Sun-God).[15]

Tammuz was none other than the son of the Great Virgin Mother and Whore-Goddess, Aphrodite—also known throughout the ancient world as Venus, Ishtar, Demeter, Meri, Isis, Astarte, Inanna, Myrrha, Artemis, Miriam, Kelle, Ninhursag, and, of course, the Virgin Mary.

The death of the Sun/Son-God was necessary in order to wash away the sins of the community and revitalize the soil for spring planting. Death was always performed in the traditional Pagan manner: by piercing or crucifixion. The blood of the Savior-Sun/Son fructifies Mother-Earth as it spills upon the ground (that is, her body).

Goddess then resurrects the dead child and mates with him,[16] an act that inaugurates her New Lunar Year, which in the Old Religion (that is the

---

14. For examples of Jesus as the Christian (biblical) Sun-God, the veritable "Sun of Righteousness," see e.g., Malachi 4:2; Isaiah 9:2, 42:6; Matthew 4:16; Luke 1:79; John 1:4, 9; 8:12; 12:35, 46; 2 Corinthians 4:6; Ephesians 5:14; 2 John 2:8; Revelation 21:23.
15. See e.g., Ezekiel 8:14.
16. This explains why so many goddesses are portrayed as both the mothers and the wives of the various Sun/Son-gods.

Goddess Faith) begins in March (the time of the Spring Equinox),[17] ruled by Aries, the "Sacred Sacrificial Lamb."

Revealingly, as we shall see, the month of March is named after the God Mars, who in turn took his name from the great prehistoric Indo-European Mother-Goddess, variously called: Ma, Ma Ma, Mar, Mara, Mari, Maria, Mariam, Marian, Marie, Maris, Mary, Maya, Meri, Miriam, the Moerae, Mu, and Myrrha.

Let us note here that the incredible frequency of the *ma*, *mar*, and *mari* elements in Goddess names derives from the connection between her salty amniotic fluid (the "source of all life"), ocean water (chemically almost identical to both menstrual blood and amniotic fluid), and the Latin word for sea, which is *mare* (the plural, seas, is *maria*).[18]

Revealingly, Catholics still refer to the Virgin Mary by one of the titles of the old Whore-Goddess Aphrodite: *Stella Maris* ("Star of the Sea").[19]

FUNCTIONS OF THE ANCIENT PROSTITUTE

The chief roles of the ancient (female) whore were to school men in the sexual mysteries and, in the process, teach them how to attain spiritual enlightenment through sex, a type of knowledge (in Greek *gnosis*) known to mystics as "The Whore Wisdom."

Not only did ancient female whores act as transmitters of the all-powerful life-giving female energy, they also kept track of the passage of the seasons, and of time itself.

In their role as temple-priestesses the Horae or Holy Whores would perform a magic ceremony, then anoint a man's phallus (euphemistically called the "head") with sacred oil (called in Greek *chrism*), and mount him to

---

17. In ancient times the Spring Equinox, around March 21, marked the beginning of the Pagan New Year. To try and kill the feminine Pagan spirit of the holiday, in 1582 Pope Gregory XIII (1502-1585) changed the New Year to January 1, where it remains to this day. That January 1 as the beginning of the "New Year" is completely counterintuitive has not gone unnoticed by the sagacious. The Pagans had it right, of course. Spring is the natural New Year, and the one still celebrated by millions around the world (including some Christians), despite the imposition of the masculine Christian calendar and the unnatural January 1 date.

18. Early on the *mare* element found its way across the Western world, resulting in such words as the Old English *mere* ("sea" or "pool"), the Old High German *meri* ("sea"), and the Old Slavic *morje* ("ocean"). From the Latin *mare* or *maria* we get such modern words as marine, marina, mariner, marinate, maritime, and mermaid.

19. Aphrodite's name itself means "[born] of the [green sea] foam." Aphrodite gave her name to the continent of Africa, and from her name we derive the word aphrodisiac. Aphrodite was not only the goddess after whom a region or nation was named. Among others, Britain, Italy, Crete, Holland, Scotland, Greece, Albania, Palestine, Denmark, Malta, Ireland, Romania, Israel, Cuba, Scandinavia, and even Europe herself, all derive from the names of ancient female deities, as do many cities, rivers, and mountains. For more on this topic see my books *Britannia Rules* and *The Book of Kelle*.

orgasm. This act, known as the Heiros Gamos ("Sacred Union"), allowed for the transfer of procreative power from female to male, since, according to Goddess tradition, men lack the ability to generate the life force (Shakti), which is only possessed by the female.

As the "caretakers of time," the ancient whore's role was primarily to aid in the construction of astrological charts, which were called "Whore-Skopus," or as we now call them, "horoscopes" (literally meaning "watcher of the hours"), named after the temple priestesses—the Horae—who guarded the "heavenly spheres of time" kept inside Goddess' Temples.

SACRALITY OF THE NUMBER THIRTEEN
So honored were the Horae that in ancient Graeco-Roman times, a festival, called the Horaea, was held every year in their name. Each temple had twelve Holy Harlots (all named "Hora"), headed by a thirteenth member: the Great Mother-Goddess herself.

The number thirteen was considered holy in accordance with Goddess' Lunar Calender, which has thirteen twenty-eight-day months in its year. (The Moon was held to be a personification of Goddess since its monthly twenty-eight-day phases correspond with a woman's monthly twenty-eight-day menstrual cycle.) In this way, the number thirteen became one of Goddess' sacred lucky numbers.

4
EVOLUTION OF THE HOLY HARLOT

THE WHORE AS VIRGIN-MOTHER

ANCIENT sacred whores were the original "Virgin Mothers" since they gave birth without the aid of men. How was this possible?

The notion of paternity (the male's role in reproduction) was then unknown (and is still unknown in some living archaic societies). Thus women were thought to be parthenogenetic, that is, "self-fertilizing" deities, a prehistoric belief that gave rise to the idea of the "virgin mother."

Since, as it was believed in the pre-scientific period, men provided no contribution to the procreative process, they were seen by women as little more than adjunct laborers, servants, guards, hunters, sexual companions, and warriors, drone-like roles which the men acted out under the authority of the great tribal clan mother and her all-female council of twelve priestesses.

THE SIN OF MONOGAMY

Not surprisingly, ancient whores saw little use for men outside of these purely utilitarian roles, which is why they rejected the notion of monogamy. They understood that, at the time, long-term monogamous relationships mainly benefitted men, who used this unnatural form of bonding to manipulate the inherently superior intellectual and sexual powers of women for their own self-serving needs.

Ancient whores were far ahead of the men of their day in this regard. For they knew, as a few wise women today know, that a woman's extraordinary multi-orgasmic response requires more stamina than one male can muster.

This is why, for thousands of years, during the Neolithic "Golden Age of Women," or what I call "The Goddess World," the great Whore-Mother-Goddess discouraged (and in some cases even seems to have prohibited) monogamy among her followers, calling it a "sin," and instead—in keeping with the biological and primatological dictates laid down by Mother-Nature—advocated polygamy.

WOMEN ON TOP: ANCIENT RELATIONSHIPS

Archaeological findings reveal that Late Paleolithic and Early Neolithic women had loose flexible relationships with men that surrounded the practices of group marriage, polyandry (a woman having multiple husbands simultaneously), mate-swapping, and consort bonding (a series of brief tenuous relationships that we now call "serial polygamy").

Yes, until the Patriarchal Takeover (4300 BCE) it was women who controlled male/female relationships, ordaining who, when, how, why, and where. This is why we find thousands of ancient stone etchings and paintings portraying women in their preferred sexual position: astride the man, where they could derive the most pleasure and control the sexual act.

LESBIANS, SPIRITUAL SISTERS, & ALL-FEMALE COMMUNITIES

Naturally lesbianism was immensely popular in ancient times, with women forming all-female island communities, and even woman-exclusive villages and cities, where great female-only schools (called Collegia, the forerunners of today's colleges) flourished.

Here, the Female Principle was venerated and the feminine arts of lesbian love, poetry, song, and dance, were taught by such famed women as Sappho. Her all-woman Greek island community, Lesbos, gives us the modern word lesbian.

On Lesbos, for example, when a woman from such a community wanted a child, or simply desired physical intimacy with the opposite gender, she would leave for the mainland to mate with the man of her choice.

Men, however, were never allowed into ancient lesbian colonies, and if caught, the punishment was castration and ritual sacrifice. This sentence was meted out by the lesbian militia, comprised of a troop of specially-trained, highly athletic Amazonian warrioresses who took no quarter, and who, according to tradition, often maimed, and even killed, men for pleasure (another reason for this was the ancient Amazonian belief that "crippled men make better lovers").

After her sojourn to the mainland the voyaging woman would return to bear and raise her infant among her female colleagues, away from the dangers and hazards of the male world.

For such women the idea of living with a man in a monogamous romantic relationship was considered a "barbarous blasphemy." The only lifestyle deemed appropriate was that of living in a close-knit community of "sisters"; a community where violence, aggression, and deception were unknown (at least toward each other), and where tenderness, maternal warmth, and compassion ruled.

This lifestyle was not just for lesbians, of course. Many thousands of heterosexual women joined these all-female communities as well. For it was only among such humanitarian-based female-exclusive groups that many women felt they could reach their full potential; a vibrant peaceful mode of living where men, with their naturally aggressive and bellicose ways, could not interfere.

THE ENDURING FEMALE RELATIONSHIP
What these ancient women were doing was keeping alive the great Sisterhood, a tradition that has existed for nearly 54 million years among our nonhuman female primate ancestors.

Here, from out of our long primate heritage,[20] we find the very heart and soul of the great matriarchies of the ancient Goddess World, a tradition that once permeated every culture, society, and religion of that age: the female-on-female bond, a relationship, whether sexual or Platonic, that is usually far more enduring (and, some would say, fulfilling) than the female-on-male bond.

It is indeed a scientifically observable fact that female-on-female friendships generally outlast female-on-male friendships, that most lesbian marriages outlast both gay and heterosexual marriages, and that mother-daughter relationships are typically more profound and long lasting than father-son relationships.[21]

---

20. See Appendix H.
21. There are, of course, exceptions. However, when it comes to relationship longevity, studies have amply shown that gay (male) marriages are typically the shortest, heterosexual marriages fall in the middle, and lesbian marriages are generally the longest.

5

WHEN JUDAISM WAS MATRIARCHAL

GODDESS-WORSHIP AMONG THE ISRAELITES

SADLY, the Goddess-worshiping Sisterhood would begin to disintegrate after the Patriarchal Takeover in 4300 BCE. Yet its influence lasted well into the historical period, intensely affecting society and religion alike.

Before Judaism became patriarchal (around 500 BCE), it was, like all of the earliest religions, matriarchal: ancient Jews worshiped the Feminine Principle, and sacred prostitution played a major function in daily temple life at Jerusalem. The custom was so popular and widespread that it had to be repeatedly banned by the new incoming patriarchal hierarchy.[22]

JEWISH WHORE WISDOM

The Whore Wisdom too was well-known among the Israelites and other early Semitic peoples, who called it the *Yada*, a Hebrew word meaning variously "teach," "understand," "perceive," and "knowledge."[23]

The "teaching," "understanding," and "perception" of *Yada*, however, does not refer to intellectual knowledge. It refers to spiritual knowledge or cosmic enlightenment, the Great Gnosis of the Whore-Goddess, whose path to its attainment is through the sex act.

Unfortunately, throughout the Old Testament Medieval English scribes misleadingly translated the Hebrew word *Yada*—and throughout the New Testament its Greek equivalent *Ginosko*—as the words "knew," "know," or "knowing." Nonetheless, the original meaning of *Yada* and *Ginosko* (that is, achieving divine illumination through sex) can still be seen in many biblical passages.[24]

---

22. See e.g., Deuteronomy 23:18.
23. See e.g., Nehemiah 10:28.
24. See e.g., in particular Genesis 3:5; but also Genesis 4:1; 38:26; 1 Kings 1:4; Matthew 1:25.

JEWISH SERPENT CULTS

Some early Hebrew males honored the Whore Wisdom so ardently that they intentionally married prostitutes. One such man was the mystic Moses, leader of an occultic Snake Cult that venerated the Hebrew Serpent-God Nehustan.[25] Moses wed a black African prostitute, angering many of his unenlightened family members.[26]

We will note here that the Greek Father-God Zeus was often worshiped in the form of a snake. Since, in Hebrew mythology, Yahweh (named after Israel's oldest deity, the Goddess Iahu) is merely a Semitic version of Zeus, it is not surprising that he was sometimes imaged by early Hebrews as a serpent as well.

Nehustan, whose name means "a piece of brass," is actually the Hebrew name for Asklepios, the ancient Greek God of Healing, whose sacred serpent can still be seen today in the symbol of modern medicine: the Caduceus (two snakes entwined around a winged staff).

It is no accident that ancient Hebrew mythology portrays Moses marrying a whore, for the early Near-Eastern serpent cults originated from out of the sex and fertility rites of prehistoric Goddess-worship (serpent-goddesses, such as Kadru, Lamia, Coatlicue, Tiamat, Hecate, Leviathan, Britomartis, Sphinx, Medusa, Morrigan, and Hydra, are plentiful in all religions), whose World Serpent lays the World Egg, which breaks open, bringing forth all life.

Goddess' sacred snake—in the Old Religion an archetypal symbol of wisdom and immortality—was demonized by patriarchal Hebrew priests, who appended it to the Hebrew Creation myth as the evil serpent that tempted Adam and Eve in the Garden of Eden.[27]

PROSTITUTION AT THE JEWISH TEMPLE

Despite such efforts, however, sacred prostitution continued on in the "House of the Lord" for centuries after, often under the name of the Semitic Whore-Goddess Ishara (Asherah to the Jews), who governed licentious behavior.

During the time of King Josiah (640-609 BCE), for instance, Jewish temple prostitutes (who venerated the great Hebrew Triple-Goddess) lived

---

25. 2 Kings 18:4; Numbers 21:6-9.
26. Numbers 12:1.
27. Genesis 3:1-15. It is interesting to note here that modern Mormons believe that the Pagan Snake-God Quetzalcoatl is actually Jesus Christ.

next to the triple-towered Jerusalem Temple, where, as the Bible tells us, they "wove hangings for the Sacred Grove of Goddess"[28] while singing to attract customers.[29] The *qadeshah*, as the consecrated temple whore was known, often sat by the side of the road offering herself in the name of Asherah.[30] Blessed was the man who partook in her sacred rites.

THE MANY NAMES OF THE JEWISH WHORE-GODDESS
Ishara the great Virgin-Whore-Mother-Goddess was known to the Israelites by many names, including: Asherah (or Ashtoreth), Ishtar, Shekhina, the Word, Hokmah, Sophia, Bath Qol, Zion, the Earth, the Community of Israel, Astarte, and Hor, words betraying a profound belief in the Divine Feminine among the early forerunners of the Jews.

As proof we have the word Israel itself, whose first syllable derives from the name of the Pagan Mother-Goddess of Egypt, Isis (note that the second syllable of the word Israel comes from the Pagan Father-God Ra, while the third syllable is from the Pagan Sacrificial Savior-Son-God El; thus Is-Ra-El).

PALESTINE, THE HORA DANCE, & THE JEWISH LUNAR CALENDER
Palestine too takes her name from a Pagan Goddess; in this case, the Roman Cattle-Goddess Pales, whose festival, the Parilia, was held in ancient Rome every year on April 21.

To this day the oldest authentic Hebrew folkdance is called "Hora," named after the zodiacal circle dances of the ancient Jewish Temple prostitutes, who maintained the "hours of time" so that horoscopes could be cast correctly, and so that seeds could be planted and harvested in their proper seasons.[31]

The modern Jewish calender, which is Moon-based, also continues to betray the influence of Goddess-worship in ancient Israel, for it was founded on the idea of the Goddess Asherah's thirteen-month, twenty-eight-day Lunar Year.

So powerful was the early Hebrew love of Goddess that Jewish priests spent centuries trying to stamp it out, as the length and breadth of the Bible so clearly shows. But all to no avail. Many modern Jewish sects, such as the Sephardim, the Oriental Jews, and the Hasidic Ashkenazim, retain strong

---

28. 2 Kings 23:7.
29. Isaiah 23:15-16.
30. Genesis 38:21-22.
31. Genesis 1:14.

elements of ancient Hebrew Goddess-worship, and Asherah's place in Judaism is once again being discussed among all manner of Jews.

JEWISH WOMEN WHO TRIED TO REVIVE GODDESS-WORSHIP
In earlier times the great Hebrew King Solomon (whose name means "Sun-God of On") was an ardent Goddess-worshiper,[32] while the Old Testament reveals that two ancient Jewish queens, Maachah and Athaliah (a daughter of Jezebel—herself a Hebrew Goddess-worshiper, and the granddaughter of Maachah) tried to revive Goddess-worship among their people, much to the displeasure of the all-male Jewish priesthood[33]—who stripped the former of her crown[34] and killed the latter.[35]

Because of her hatred of the Father-God Yahweh,[36] as well as her love of Goddess and her practice of worshiping Goddess in her sacred tree groves,[37] Jezebel was not only called a "whore" and a "witch" by patriarchal Hebrew priests, but she too was cruelly murdered.[38]

Right into the present time Jezebel's name remains a pejorative term in our patriarchal culture, one used to mean a "shameless," "impudent," or "abandoned" woman; in other words, a whore.

But Jezebel need not have felt shame, and we can be sure that she did not. For among the female Goddess-worshipers of that day there was no higher calling than working as a sacred prostitute in the local temple.

THE SEMITIC GODDESS HOR & THE VULVA-WORSHIPING HORITES
An entire Semitic culture, the "Horites," claimed descent from the Goddess Hor,[39] whose great holy mountain, Mount Hor,[40] stood as a maternal symbol of her life-nurturing female breasts, her magical pregnant abdomen, her round child-bearing hips, her arching buttocks, and her swollen life-giving vulva.

---

32. 1 Kings 11:5.
33. 1 Kings 15:10-13; 2 Kings 11:1-20.
34. 1 Kings 15:13.
35. 2 Kings 11:20.
36. 1 Kings 18:4.
37. 1 Kings 30-33.
38. 2 Kings 9:22-37.
39. Genesis 14:6.
40. Numbers 20:23.

The ancient Romans called the latter body part *Mons Veneris* ("Mound of Venus") after their own version of Hor, the Love- and Sex-Goddess Venus. Venus was known in Phoenicia as the Goddess Mylitta or Mu'Allidtu. Here, Mylitta's female followers offered themselves to this "Goddess of Desire" by having sacred sex with strangers in private booths near her shrines.

The Horites' name refers to their custom of living in caves (symbols of the dark moist magical vulva of Goddess), evidence of a profound Whore-Mother religion in early Palestine. The Horites were in fact Yoni-worshipers, whose Cult of the Vulva was banned when Judaism was finally patricized by misogynistic Jewish priests in the 6th Century BCE.

Today the Horites are variously referred to as the "Hurrians," "Hittites," or "Hivites." These modern appellations, however, cannot obscure the true nature of the ancient Horites, for the early Jews called them the *Hori*, a word that literally means "cave-dweller," or occultly, "vulva-worshipers."

THE CREATION OF THE WHORE OF BABYLON
Following the Jewish male demonization of prostitution, and of women in general, Jews no longer referred to Goddess by her once beloved sacred Hebrew title: "The Great Mother-Harlot of the World." Now she was disparagingly called "Mystery, Babylon, the Great Mother of Harlots"[41] and "the Great Whore which did corrupt the earth with her fornication."[42] Her followers were simply called "sodomites."[43]

DESTRUCTION OF THE MATRIARCHATE BY PATRIARCHAL JUDAISM
In their attempt to obliterate the woman-centered, matrifocal world, patriarchal Jewish priests also renamed the holy temple of the whores, calling it *Bet Boshet* ("House of Shame"); Goddess' sacred number, thirteen, was reversed to mean "bad luck"; female followers of Goddess ("witches") were ordered to be put to death;[44] and the red erect phallus signs of ancient Rome, once used to direct customers to the city's prostitutes, became signs of disgrace (the red-light of the modern whorehouse descends from this custom).

---

41. Revelation 17:5.
42. Revelation 19:2. See also 17:1, 15-16.
43. 1 Kings 22:46.
44. Exodus 22:18.

Goddess' inverted pubic triangle symbol (▽) was blotted out by placing it under an upward pointing triangle (△), the mystical symbol of the erect Male Principle. The result was the hexagramic symbol of Judaism, now called the "Star of David," or "Solomon's Seal" (✡). Yet, to mystical Jews it remains an arcane symbol of the union of the Female and Male Principles.

The "missionary position" was introduced as a way to force women into a sexually submissive role, and the great lesbian communities, all-female colleges, female-headed matriarchies, peaceful and equalitarian gylanies, and women-only island villages of the ancient world, were closed down and dismantled. By the mid 5th Millennium BCE, the circle of the great global Sisterhood had finally been broken.

Though Goddess and her religion hung on in various manifestations (for example, she was often now portrayed as the mere mate of the male Supreme Being rather than as the Supreme Being herself), with the arrival of orthodox Christianity in the early centuries of the Common Era, the Whore-Mother-Goddess' temples were ordered completely destroyed; or, more often, converted into Christian churches.

This anti-woman, anti-Goddess campaign of terror was enthusiastically embraced and aggressively advocated by numerous early Church Fathers, including Saint Paul.[45]

---

[45]. Acts 19:27.

6
ARCHETYPES, FATHERS, & POLYGAMY

THE INVINCIBLE WHORE-MOTHER

ULTIMATELY the Great Whore Wisdom (a tradition carried on today by mystics of all religions), and more particularly the love of whores themselves, could not be killed off, or even suppressed by Christian authorities.

As psychologists well-know, the maternal figure (with her great oceanic "motherly love" for her worldwide family) is the psychic nucleus of not only all personal human relationships, but of human society itself.

In addition, all women naturally possess the prostitute-maternal archetype within themselves, an archetype that Sigmund Freud referred to as the "Whore-Madonna Complex."

As is clear, archetypes cannot be eradicated. They are eternal, for they are biologically and spiritually embedded in the body and soul of every human.

MEN GENERALLY MAKE POOR HUSBANDS & FATHERS

On the other hand, neither paternal love, paternity, or the paternal figure played vital roles in human society until after 10,000 BCE, at which time paternity was first discovered (through the domestication of wild animals).[46] For reasons which we have discussed, "fatherhood," as Margaret Mead and other anthropologists have repeatedly observed, is a "recent cultural invention."

This explains why among almost every known people, numerous social, legal, civil, financial, and religious laws have been created to entice, or even coerce, men into marriage—*and* keep them there.

---

[46]. So that there is no misunderstanding here, I am saying that while *men* did play important roles, *fathers* did not. The difference is enormous. This view, which is shared by others, is based on a careful study of the fossil record, nonhuman primates, and living archaic human societies.

The truth is that neither long-term monogamous marriage, the two-parent family unit, or the role of father are natural to men. And so these newly created cultural ideas must be intentionally (and often quite forcibly) taught to males from an early age. Without this intensive socialization for family life, few men would find this mode of living inviting, or even tolerable.

COERCING MEN INTO MONOGAMOUS MARRIAGE

So strong is the vagabond-hunter programming in men that even when they are both socialized for matrimony and pressured with strict regulations and sanctions, most eventually rebel against it, either through various forms of physical, mental, verbal, and emotional abuse, or by way of infidelity, desertion, and divorce.

Indeed, the divorce rate in Western countries is around 60 percent, while the male infidelity rate is around 80 percent. And both figures are rising annually.

What all of this tells us is that there is a great underlying and inherent dissatisfaction among the majority of men toward lifelong monogamous marriage.

WOMEN ARE NATURALLY POLYGAMOUS

It should be pointed out here that lifelong, or even long-term, monogamy is not natural to women either: this type of bond has never occurred at any time in human evolution (that is, until the emergence of Christianity, 2,000 years ago).[47] Therefore it is clear that neither modern women or men are genetically adapted for it.

However, due to the female's maternal instincts—which are based on the female's more malleable and compassionate emotional and psychological

---

47. The ancient pre-Christian Romans did practice a form of monogamous marriage. But it was loosely defined, divorce was allowed, and husbands were permitted to visit prostitutes. This is not *lifelong* monogamy.

make-up and greater thinking capacity[48]—family life is generally more bearable for her than it is for a man.

Nonetheless, the facts are, as the latest studies indicate, that not only are women usually the ones to file for divorce first, at least 70 percent of all married women cheat on their husbands, revealing that women's freedom-loving polygamous urges are just as strong as they were in prehistoric times; a time when women fulfilled their sexual needs by practicing group marriage, polyandry, polyamory, lesbianism, and serial polygamy.

---

48. The corpus callosum (a band of tissue—often likened to an electrical cable—that connects the two hemispheres of the brain) is significantly thicker in human females than in human males. This does not in any way make women smarter. But, on average, it does seem to allow them to think faster and process more thoughts at one time than men. This biological phenomenon, a product of millions of years of evolution (which, contrary to the teachings of radical feminists, designed women to be maternal caregivers and men to be big-game hunters), tends to make women better multitaskers and men more single-minded. These traits suited our prehistoric male and female ancestors perfectly, of course. How well they suit us modern humans (in a world where men no longer need to hunt large dangerous animals to survive and women now do far more than bear and care for children) is a matter of great conjecture and widely varying opinion.

7
MARY & THE CHRISTIAN PATRIARCHAL TAKEOVER

THE PAGANIZATION OF MARY & JESUS

SOON realizing that they were up against an irresistible force (that is, both biology and the innate human love of the Mother Archetype), the early Church Fathers finally accepted the fact that they could not exterminate the Great Virgin Whore-Mother. We will recall that this was a deity whom much of the ancient Indo-European world knew by some variation of the name "Mari."[49]

Their solution? According to a careful study of the evolution of Christian mythology, they simply transformed her into the "Virgin Mary"—or perhaps they appended many of Mari's traits to the historical Mary. Additionally, Mari's sacrificial Divine Son, the Pagan Savior Hesus (known to Jews as Tammuz),[50] was recast as Jesus (whose name is, in part, a hebracization of the name of the Pagan Greek Savior-God-King, Jason).[51]

---

49. As mentioned, owing to the Divine Feminine's occultic and symbolic connection to the sea (in Latin, *mare*), many goddesses around the world have been given names with the *ma* or *mar* element in them. For example: Ma, Ma Ma, Mar, Mara, Mari, Maria, Mariam, Marian, Marie, Maris, Mary, Maya, Meri, Miriam, the Moerae, Mu, and Myrrha. Aphrodite, the Great Whore-Goddess herself, often went by the title *Stella Maris* ("Star of the Sea").

50. Besides Hesus and Tammuz, there were thousands of other Christs; that is, sacrificial saviors and son-gods, that pre-dated Christianity. Among them: Adad, Antheus, Attis, Baal, Bacchus, Balili, Balder, Bali, Beddru, Belenus, Buddha, Bunjil, Chrishna (Krishna), Criti, Cyrus, Dionysus, Eros, Glooskap, Horus, Hyacinth, Indra, Ieoud, Iva, Jao, Jason, Jesus ben Pandira, Joshua, Kukulcan, Liber Pater, Lleu Llaw Gyffes, Lugh, Mahavira, Marduk, Mikado, Mitra, Mithra, Mithras, Odin, Orontes, Osiris, Pan, Pentheus, Prometheus, Quetzalcoatl, Sabazius, Sakia, Saoshyant, Shemesh, Son of Man, Son of Righteousness, Thor, Thules, Witoba, Woden, Zagreus, Zalmoxis, and Zoroastra.

51. Note that I am not saying here that Jesus was not a historical person. What I am saying is that his figure and life story were (tragically) later paganized by the early Christian Church (that is, the Catholic Church). For more on this topic, see my book *Christmas Before Christianity: How the Birthday of the "Sun" Became the Birthday of the "Son."*

GODDESS' CHRISTING RITUAL

The word "Christ," meaning "the anointed," was derived from the Horae's sacred sexual oil called *chrism*, which means "to anoint." The Goddess christing ritual predates Christianity by thousands of years, and was even commonly used by the Israelites,[52] sometimes in male homosexual rites.[53]

The occultic secret behind the word *chrism* is that it is often used in the Bible as a euphemism for the male sexual fluid, semen. This becomes more apparent when we study the original Hebrew word for Goddess' christing oil, which is *shemen*.[54] Unhappily, these facts have been obscured by misunderstanding, fear, ignorance, and mistranslation, preventing millions from advancing in their spiritual growth.

Nonetheless, the connection between Goddess, her christing ritual, and her child, the Sun/Son-God, is patently obvious when we use etymology to uncover the hidden or esoteric meaning of the word chrism. Chrism, in fact, derives from the ancient Chaldean word *chrs* or—with vowels—*chris* (in Hebrew written *heres* or *hrs*), meaning the "Sun," an overt allusion to the Pagan Savior-Son-God and his role as a solar deity (that is, a Sun-God).

CHRISTIANIZATION OF THE TRIPLE-GODDESS

The Church Fathers stole, adopted, and christianized many other items from Goddess' Old Religion. For instance, the great Indo-European Triple-Goddess Mari, the original Pagan Holy Trinity, who mourned at the foot of the tree upon which her Divine Son-God had been executed, was transformed into both the three "Marys" who stood at the foot of Jesus' cross,[55] and the masculinized "Holy Trinity" of the "Father, Son, and Holy Ghost."[56]

Mari's mother, the Pagan Crone-Goddess Anna, was "borrowed" by the Church as well, becoming the fictitious "Saint Anne." According to her fabricated Christian legend, Saint Anne was said to have given birth to three daughters, all named "Mary," another overt christianization of the Pagan Triple-Goddess Mari.

---

52. Exodus 30:30-31.
53. Psalms 89:20.
54. See e.g., the original Hebrew word for "oil" in Exodus 30:25.
55. John 19:25.
56. Matthew 28:19. After the Christian theft and adoption of the Pagan Trinity idea, it took many decades, even centuries, to fully develop it, which is why Paul, writing in the mid 1st Century, knew nothing of it and does not once mention the Trinity in any of his authentic letters.

Goddess' sacred bird, the peaceful dove, was appended to the figure of the strangely feminine but genderless "Holy Ghost,"[57] while Goddess and her Twelve Temple Harlots were masculinized and overlaid upon the figures of Jesus and his Twelve Disciples—though thirteen remained a number associated with bad luck. (To this day, many multistoried buildings have no thirteenth floor, and the phrase "a baker's dozen" allows the superstitious to avoid the use of the word thirteen.)

MARY MAGDALENE & THE WHORE WISDOM

The ancient Pagan Whore Wisdom too was adopted and christianized by the authors of the New Testament, where it is personified in the temple-whore figure of "Mary Magdalene" (Magdalene literally means "she of the temple-power"). This is why it is Magdalene who is portrayed as "christing" Jesus as a Pagan king in the manner of a Holy Whore: by anointing his head with sacred oil.[58]

The human head, of course, is a mystical symbol of the head of the phallus (which is why anointing normally took place on the "head"),[59] while Jesus' royal crown is, in turn, an occult circular symbol of the vulva, which the male organ must penetrate in order for the sacred female energy (the "temple-power") to be transmitted to the male.

As the Gnostic work *The Gospel of Mary* implies, the whore Mary Magdalene and a group of (twelve) women are shown financially and spiritually supporting Jesus and the Twelve Apostles during their ministry,[60] since men lack Shakti; that is, the procreative life-force.

Mary Magdalene and her Twelve Holy Harlots are also depicted as the first to visit the womb-cave of Goddess into which the body of Goddess' divine son Hesus or Jesus was laid after his crucifixion.[61]

Jesus' *three days* in the womb-cave[62] derives from the fact that there are three days between the phases of the Crone-Goddess (the Old Moon) and the phase of the Virgin-Goddess (the New Moon). It is at this time that the Mother-Goddess (the Dark Moon) appears to be "dead," after which she is

---

57. Matthew 3:16.
58. Matthew 26:7-12.
59. See e.g., Psalms 23:5.
60. For the canonical version, see Luke 8:1-3.
61. Luke 23:55-56; 24:1-10.
62. Matthew 27:57-60.

"born again" or "resurrected" on the third day. It is clear that this part of Goddess' Savior-Son legend was also appended to the story of Jesus.[63]

As mentioned, Magdalene was also the first to see and speak to the risen Savior, a necessary act which—according to mystical feminine tradition—revitalizes the inherently deficient male with the female force.[64]

Here, the Temple Whores are shown mourning for Jesus, just as earlier Jewish women mourned outside the Jerusalem Temple for the dead Syrian Savior Tammuz,[65] another of the many pre-Christian saviors who served as a prototype for the development of the Pagan aspects of the historical figure of Jesus.

JESUS & MARY MAGDALENE: THE ROYAL BLOODLINE

Jesus—himself the biological descendant of a long and ancient line of prostitutes (including Thamar, Rachab, Ruth, and Bathseheba)[66]—is said to have passed his royal blood (or, in Old French, *sang réal*) down into the modern day world through a whore.[67] We are speaking here again of Mary Magdalene.

According to Gnostic Christian tradition, ancient documents hint at a secret marriage between Jesus and Mary Magdalene in Cana of Galilee,[68] one that produced a daughter named Sarah (Hebrew for "Princess")—later known in Christian mythology as "Saint Sarah."

After Jesus' death and resurrection, Mary Magdalene and Sarah are said to have traveled across the Mediterranean Sea to the South of France (in a boat with no sails or oars), where they settled into the local community. Here they were embraced (and protected) by French royalty. After Mary died, Sarah married into one of these blue-blooded families and bore children.

Gnostic Christian documents purporting to contain Jesus' family tree reveal that around the year 400, one of Sarah's female descendants, Basina, Princess of the Thuringians and the wife of Clodion, King of France, became impregnated by a fish, called a "Quinotaur," while swimming in the ocean.

---

63. Matthew 27:62-64; Luke 24:6-7.
64. John 20:1-18.
65. Ezekiel 8:14.
66. For the names of some of the whores in Jesus' family tree, see e.g., Matthew 1, verses 3 (Thamar), 5 (Rachab and Ruth), and 6 (Bathsheba, the "wife of Urias").
67. It is interesting to note that the French phrase *san gréal* means "Holy Grail." Pertaining to the life story of Jesus, much confusion has come from the similarity of this term and *sang réal*, "royal blood." For more on this topic, see Baigent, Leigh, and Lincoln, *Holy Blood, Holy Grail*.
68. This marriage is mystically hidden in John 2:1-2.

The fish, being the ancient symbol of Jesus (who ruled the Age of Pisces, symbolized by two fish), seems to have been used in these documents to conceal the truth about Jesus and Mary Magdalene from all but the most religiously educated and spiritually enlightened.

The son born (about the year 415) of this union between Basina and the mysterious "fish" was none other than Merovech the Young, who became King of France (447-458), and whose name marks the beginning of the Divine Royal Bloodline of Jesus and Mary Magdalene in Europe.[69]

Merovech, or Merovee as he is also known, gave his name to the Merovingians, a fascinating dynasty of long-haired Frankish kings, said to have been adepts in the occult mysteries, possessing amazing curative powers (crystal balls, golden bull heads, miniature golden bees, and such, have been found in Merovingian tombs).

While the Gnostic *Gospel of Philip* tells us that "Christ loved Mary Magdalene more than all the disciples and used to kiss her often on her mouth,"[70] concrete evidence for Jesus' marriage to the prostitute is not easy to come by, for most of it has been thoroughly suppressed, or obfuscated, over the centuries by patriarchal Catholic authorities, as it was in the book of John (2:1-2).

HOW DA VINCI PRESERVED THE DIVINE FEMININE

Besides this single New Testament reference, one of the more intriguing remaining vestiges comes from Leonardo da Vinci, who was a member of the Illuminati, or Priory of Scion, an occultic organization sworn to maintain, and also pass along, the secret knowledge (gnosis) of the marriage of Jesus and his whore-bride.

One of the methods da Vinci used to hand this sacred information down to later generations was through his artwork, the best known example being his painting *The Last Supper*. Here we clearly see a woman sitting on Jesus' right side. Could this, a mysterious and unnamed figure known as "the Beloved Disciple" of the fourth Gospel,[71] be Mary Magdalene?

Over the years the painting seems to have been tampered with (by patriarchalists) in an attempt to extinguish, or at least obscure, the truth about this intriguing female and her connection to Jesus. But such feeble attempts to hide the Whore Wisdom are doomed to failure.

---

69. Merovech is my 49th great-grandfather.
70. Gospel of Philip, verse 59.
71. John 13:23.

GOD BEGAN AS GODDESS

Despite centuries of violent anti-Goddess, anti-woman pogroms, and pious anti-prostitution edicts by the Jewish and Christian patriarchies, the attempt to suppress the Great Whore-Mother-Goddess, her Whore Wisdom, and her global Society and Church—known as the Matriarchate—ultimately miscarried. Why?

Realizing that humanity's psychic need for an all-giving, life-nurturing maternal figure is indestructible, the early Church Fathers simply merged Goddess and her three primary personifications (Grandmother, Mother, and Daughter) with three popular patriarchal figures:

1) the new male Jewish supreme deity named "Jah,"[72] or rather "Yahweh"[73]
2) Jesus[74]
3) the Holy Ghost[75]

It is not surprising to learn then that the etymology of the word "Yahweh" (or "Jehovah," as Christians call him) actually means "the eternal union of the Female and Male Principles."

GODDESS-WORSHIP IN THE OLD TESTAMENT

Still, traces of a time when Judaism was a matriarchal Goddess-worshiping religion are abundant, no more so than in the Bible itself.

In the book of Psalms, for instance, ancient Jewish mythographers and scribes accidentally left in what some today believe is a reference to their male "God" as the original female Goddess, an inevitable carry-over from the days when the Supreme Being was viewed by Jews not as male, but as female.[76]

Additional evidence for a once-thriving Goddess-worshiping Jewish religion may also be found in the many biblical references to God as a maternal, nurturing, homemaking, pregnant, birthing, and nursing mother.[77]

---

72. Psalms 68:4.
73. Yahweh takes his name from the far older Semitic Moon-Goddess Yareah or Iahu. See e.g., the original Hebrew in 2 Kings 23:5.
74. See e.g., Galatians 4:19.
75. See e.g., John 3:6.
76. See Psalms 48:3.
77. See e.g., Isaiah 42:14; Deuteronomy 32:18; Numbers 11:12-13.

Indeed, the Jewish creation legend of Genesis, in which God "broods upon the face of the waters,"[78] and then "gives birth" to the Universe and all life in it, is a masculinized version of the 10,000 year-old Neolithic Creation Myth in which the Great Whore-Goddess is the one and only Supreme Being, whose freely-given compassion spawns all living creatures from her oceanic amniotic fluid.

On close inspection we also find evidence in the Bible for Hebrew matrilocal marriage,[79] Hebrew matrilineality,[80] and separate living quarters for women and men,[81] one of Goddess' more important commandments to her followers.

There are even references to the Mother-Goddess Asherah (sometimes referred to esoterically as "the community of Israel") as the wife of the Father-God Yahweh,[82] Hebrew women wearing crescent-Moon shaped amulets,[83] and a birth from out of the womb of Goddess—masculinized here as "God."[84]

For those who still doubt, the Bible tells us that Israel herself was founded, not by men, but by two women: Rachel and Leah[85]—which helps explain why the word Israel contains (and begins with) the name of the great Egyptian Mother-Goddess Isis.[86]

THE GOLDEN AGE OF WOMEN: NO TRACE OF GOD
Knowing that Judaism began as a Goddess-worshiping matriarchal faith makes it easier to understand, as archaeological evidence reveals, that Goddess is not only far older than God, but that God himself is little more than a male-created composite-deity, one that came to life only when the Holy Mother was transformed into the "Holy Father" by women-hating Jewish priests.

---

78. Genesis 1:1. Here the original Hebrew word *rachaph*, meaning "to brood," has been intentionally and incorrectly translated as the modern English word "moved."
79. Genesis 2:24; 28; 29.
80. Genesis 36:1-5.
81. Esther 2:3,9; Genesis 31:33; 1 Kings 7:8.
82. Isaiah 50:1; 54:1-8.
83. Isaiah 3:18. Note: while there are many symbols of Goddess, the lunar crescent has always been the most popular.
84. Isaiah 44:2.
85. Ruth 4:11.
86. As noted earlier, the word Israel, or Is-Ra-El, derives from the names of three deities: Isis; the Egyptian Father-God Ra; and the Semitic Son-God El.

Indeed, from 500,000 BCE to 10,000 BCE—a period known as the "Golden Age of Women"—not a single representation of a male deity, man-like supreme being, or even a simple father-figure, has ever been found in the art, artifacts, or fossil remains of prehistoric peoples.

Stunningly, during this same time period, thousands of statuettes, paintings, carvings, and etchings of Goddess the Great Whore-Mother—along with numerous primitive feminine symbols (such as her inverted vulvaic triangle)—have been found in archaeological digs all over the world.

If God came before Goddess (as patriarchalists teach), why are there no hints of his existence or worship during this immense span of time?

THE PATRIARCHAL TAKEOVER: FROM EARTH-MOTHER TO SKY-FATHER

The answer is simple: early peoples did not recognize the human male as possessing divine power. Only the female. Thus, only Woman was deified.

As scientists, like social anthropologist Robert S. Briffault and archaeologist Marija A. Gimbutas, have shown, the deification of men, and the ensuing creation of the "Father-God," would have to wait until the Patriarchal Takeover, a world-altering event in which thousands of horse-back-riding patriarchal warriors swept across matriarchal Europe from out of southern Russia some 6,000 years ago.

These Aryans (or Kurgans or Indo-Europeans, as they are also known) crushed the great matriarchies, drove women from their thrones, and stole women's political, legal, economic, sexual, civil, educational, familial, and reproductive powers for themselves. In place of the feminine Goddess, the Aryans created and worshiped a deity molded in their own image; namely, a masculine God.

From out of this period was created the first known male deity, one closely associated, not with vegetation, the harvest, or the female Earth, but with thunder, rain, and the male Sun. In this way religion went from a matrifocal belief-system based on worship of the Earth-Mother, to a patrifocal belief-system based on the veneration of the Sky-Father.

To this day many men still search for their God (that is, science-based humanism, rational materialism, and logical positivism) by shooting phallic rockets into the heavens, while at the same time they show disrespect for Goddess by scarring and raping her body (the Earth) with machines and pollutants.

8
CHRISTIANITY'S SACRED WHORES

HOW THE CHANGING NAMES OF GOD REVEAL HIS WHORE-GODDESS ROOTS

THE invention of the figure of the father-god is so recent that when Moses met the Judeo-Christian "God" in a burning bush (said to have taken place around 3,000 years ago), the patriarch had no idea what name to address him by. When Moses inquired as to the deity's name, it merely replied: "call me I AM."[87]

Later, God admitted to Moses that he was not known by name to Abraham, Isaac, or Jacob either.[88] In fact, the earliest mention of God's name in the Bible is not "God," "Yahweh," or "Jehovah." It is *El Shaddai*, a name-phrase purposefully mistranslated throughout the entire Bible by later Medieval English scribes as "the Almighty."[89]

In the earliest passages of Genesis, God is simply referred to as *Elohim*, an ancient Pagan Semitic phrase-word meaning "a council of deities." Why?

Early Jews (that is, the Hebrews) were polytheistic, and embraced the patriarchal Pagan idea that the Universe was ruled by an assembly of twelve astrological male gods and their all-powerful leader.[90] Some early Hebrews even went as far as to refer to the head of this group (that is, "God") by his Pagan name, *Baal*, meaning "father," one of the earliest Hebrew names for God.[91]

Hebrew/Jewish priests adopted and incorporated this polytheistic belief into Hebrew mythology from various Pagan religions of the day, such as the Greeks, who held that the world was governed by Zeus (to the Romans, Jupiter, or *Iu-Pater*, meaning "Heavenly Father") and his Twelve Titans. The name Zeus (like Jupiter, meaning "Sky-Father") was once used by Jews for

---

87. Exodus 3:13-14.
88. Exodus 6:3.
89. See e.g., Genesis 17:1.
90. See e.g., Joshua 24:2, 14-15; Hosea 3:1.
91. Joshua 2:16.

their Supreme God before he was given the name "Yahweh," as ancient writers such as Plutarch and Valerius Maximus have noted.

Finally, Yahweh would be given the name that he is generally known by today: God. But even this name was derived from the great Whore-Mother-Goddess.

The word God comes from the ancient Pagan Germanic word for Goddess in her Teutonic form: Goden (or Goda), the sacred consort of the German high-god Woden, who gave his name to the fourth day of our week, Woden's Day, or as we now call it, "Wednesday."[92]

When Judaism became monotheistic (an idea which the early Hebrews borrowed from the ancient Egyptian religion of the Pagan Sun-God Aton, instigated by the 18th-Dynasty Pharaoh Akhenaten in the year 1367 BCE), the Jewish Father-God (Yahweh/Jehovah) was stripped of his polytheistic attributes, at which time he became a singular high-god. It was in this period that he was given his first *Hebrew* name: El Shaddai.

WHY GOD WAS FIRST CALLED EL SHADDAI
Just what does this name mean?

El is an ancient Pagan, Semitic, gender-neutral word meaning "a magnificent deity." *Shaddai* is an ancient Pagan Semitic word meaning "the milk-giving breast," or "the nursing mother." Thus, El Shaddai literally means: the "Glorious Mother-Goddess."

Indeed, originally El Shaddai was one of the many name-titles of the Great Whore-Mother herself in the form of a mountain-goddess. (We will recall that the mountain is a female breast symbol, and is thus an emblem of Goddess' maternal, nurturing, outward-pouring, all-embracing love; that is, the "milk of human kindness").

THE WHORE-GODDESS AS CHRISTIAN SAINT
Realizing that they would have to keep the maternal energy of the Female Principle alive in order to maintain a strong church membership, Medieval Christian mythographers also parlayed the Whore-Goddess into dozens of bogus female saints, all tellingly made the "patrons of prostitutes."

Among these were "Saint Aphrodite" (an overt christianization of the Greek Sex-Goddess and Whore-Mother Aphrodite, after whom this book is named); "Saint Maudline" (yet another christianization of Mary

---

92. "Lady Godiva" is an English version of the German Goddess Goda. Lady Godiva, despite her seemingly legendary status, was a real historical person, and is, in fact, my 31st great-grandmother.

Magdalene); and the three sisters known variously as "Saint Irene," "Saint Agape," and "Saint Chionia"; or as "Saint Hope," "Saint Faith," and "Saint Charity." All were said to be the daughters of the equally spurious "Saint Sophia."

In truth Saint Sophia herself is but a christianization of the Grecian Whore-Wisdom-Goddess Sophia (the word *sophia* is Greek for "wisdom"), while Saint Chionia, Saint Agape, and Saint Irene, were nothing more than christianizations of the three far older Pagan Holy Whores, the Charites, or Horae named: *Eunomia* ("Good Order"), *Dike* ("Justice"), and *Eirene* ("Peace").

Masculine-like lesbians are today still affectionately called "dykes" in honor of the whore-goddess Dike, though the term is used disparagingly by homophobes.

MINNE, THE CULT OF MARY, & THE CHRISTIAN WHOREHOUSE

Overt worship of the Great Whore-Goddess continued on into the Middle Ages, growing in intensity with the passing centuries.

The Troubadours, for instance, worshiped the Whore-Goddess under her new Medieval name, Minne ("love"), while at the same time the Catholic Cult of Mary (as we have seen, a christianization of the Cult of the Near-Eastern Whore-Goddess Mari) had by then become more popular than the Cult of Jesus. (This trend continues in the Catholic Church to this day—much to the shock and chagrin of the all-male Church hierarchy—a natural result of the human preference for, and attraction to, the archetypal maternal figure).

The original whorehouses of ancient Italy, named "Abbeys" (from the Aramaic word *abba*, "father") after the "sugar daddies" who owned them, were transformed into nunneries by the Catholic Fathers. The head nun took the title "the Abbess" from the Italian madams who ran them.

Several of the more worldly Medieval popes maintained brothels (cleverly disguised as convents) in Rome, a practice that brought in more money and riches than all of the other sources of Church income combined. Among the numerous popes who both kept brothels and visited prostitutes were Sixtus IV (12th century), Innocent IV (13th century), and Leo X (16th century). There were many others.

CHRISTIANITY ONCE SUPPORTED PROSTITUTION

Actually, some of the early Church Fathers had a very practical attitude about Aphrodite's Trade. As we have seen, the sagacious Saint Augustine, as just one example, believed that prostitution served as an important social outlet, one that helped preserve marriage. (It was Augustine who once prayed: "Please God, make me celibate. But not yet.")

And in this the famed theologian was not only correct, but far ahead of his time, for modern studies do indeed show that wherever prostitution is suppressed, divorce rates go up, and wherever it is encouraged (or at least disregarded), divorce rates go down. This fact is so important, let us repeat it: *wherever prostitution is suppressed, divorce rates go up, and wherever it is encouraged (or at least disregarded), divorce rates go down.*

The reason for this is that modern monogamous marriage grew out of the prostitutionary relationships of our prehistoric ancestors (food for sex, sex for food).

One can say with good reason then that prostitution exists because of monogamous marriage, and that monogamous marriage exists because of prostitution. If one disappeared, so would the other. Monogamous marriage and prostitution are truly symbiotic.

This is why in polygamous societies prostitution is virtually nonexistent. For prostitution is rendered completely unnecessary when polygamy is present. The world's oldest profession only flourishes in the midst of monogamy.

THE U.S. ARMY LEGALIZES PROSTITUTION

There are other even more practical reasons for decriminalizing prostitution. For example, in America in 1864, during Lincoln's War, or what we here in the South call "the War for Southern Independence,"[93] the U.S. army, under General Robert Granger, legalized prostitution in order to prevent the spread of disease. For despite the army's best efforts to run thousands of working girls out of cities like Nashville, Tennessee, nothing could prevent them from eventually returning, or prevent soldiers from willingly paying for their services.

As the Catholic Church itself did at one time, the Yankee army finally capitulated, realizing that the best course of action would be to sanction and control prostitution.

The idea succeeded.

Female prostitutes were examined by Union army surgeons for venereal disease. Those who were uninfected were licensed and allowed to carry on

---

93. This conflict is widely and incorrectly known as the American "Civil War." For the authentic facts on this topic see my book *Everything You Were Taught About the Civil War is Wrong, Ask a Southerner!*

their trade. Those who were found infected were first treated and then licensed.

Using nothing more than logical thinking and common sense, the U.S. army cured thousands of women of disease, while at the same time preventing it from spreading to thousands of soldiers—whose lives and marriages would have been forever ruined.

9
COMMERCIAL PROSTITUTION & MODERN MARRIAGE

THE CREATION OF SECULAR PROSTITUTION
SACRED prostitution still carries on in a few regions of the world, most notably in India. Nearly everywhere else, however, it has been completely replaced by secular commercial prostitution, an invention of patriarchal men intent on controlling women and wiping out the sacrality of the Female Principle.

How different this is from the ancient Goddess World, where all forms of female prostitution were embedded in religion, and hence were considered extremely sacred.

In the 1990s in the U.S. alone, secular prostitution generated some $1 billion dollars every thirty days, a sum paid to 4 million working female prostitutes by 6 million clients monthly. These figures are climbing each year as prostitutes (and women from every other branch of the sex work industry) grow increasingly in demand and popularity.

MODERN CHRISTIAN WORSHIP OF THE GREAT WHORE
Even the patriarchal attempt to obliterate the Divine Feminine and the Great Whore-Goddess by secularizing prostitution has been unsuccessful. The majority of Catholics, for example, still prefer praying to the Virgin Mary rather than to Jesus, which is why it is her statue, and not Christ's, that stands in front of most Catholic churches.

Much of the figure of the historical Mary, as we have seen, is little more than a modern christianization of the Great Whore-Goddess Aphrodite as *Stella Maris* ("Star of the Sea"), the deity who ruled prostitution in ancient

Greece, and one of whose many titles was Porne (the "Harlot").[94] Her title appears numerous times (in the original Greek) throughout the New Testament.[95]

Also popularly called the "Queen of Heaven," Aphrodite was known to the Babylonians as Ishtar-Mari ("Star of the Sea"), to the Phoenicians as Astarte ("Star"), to Hindus as Kali-Meri ("Black Sea-Goddess"), to Arabs as Atthar ("Morning Star"), to Scandinavians as Frigga ("Love"), to the Celts as Kelle ("Cave" or "Hole"),[96] to the Egyptians as Isis ("She of the Throne"), to Northern Europeans as Freya ("the Lady"), to the Anatolians as Anath (the "Answer"), to the Romans as Juno ("Queenly"), and to the Israelites as Asherah ("Universal Law").[97]

That the Virgin Mary is one and the same with the above named goddesses is incontestable: as the archetypal Virgin Mother, Ishtar-Mari, for instance, gave parthenogenic birth to her Divine Savior-Son Tammuz each year on December 25, and after his sacrificial death at the Spring Equinox, Hebrew women mourned his passing at the Jerusalem Temple.[98]

As the Great Whore-Goddess, Ishtar-Mari educated her male followers in the holy Tantric mysteries by way of her sacred temple prostitutes. Thus arose one of her many names, Har, and one of her many titles, "the Mother of Harlots," demonized by early Catholic authorities as the "Great Whore of Babylon."[99]

While most Catholics are completely unaware that they are praying to a version of the Pagan Mother-Goddess, numerous other Christian denominations, primarily the Gnostics and the Shakers, openly embrace the idea of a feminine Supreme Being, while some, like the Quakers and the Unitarians, are not opposed to it.

Some of the pseudo-Christian faiths (that is, non-Bible based "Christian" churches) still worship the Mother-Goddess—though not publicly. The best known from this group are the Mormons (the Church of Jesus Christ of Latter-Day Saints, or LDS), a denomination that actually takes its name from a goddess, in this case the ancient Greek Underworld-Goddess known as

---

94. The word pornography thus means the "writing of harlots." Like nearly everything else associated with the Great Whore-Goddess Aphrodite, this once sacred word too has been demonized. According to Webster, pornography now means "erotic material intended to cause sexual excitement."
95. See e.g., 1 Corinthians 6:15-16; Hebrews 11:31; James 2:25.
96. See my work *The Book of Kelle*.
97. For an example of the early Jewish Goddess-worship of the Queen of Heaven Aphrodite as Asherah, see Jeremiah 7:18; 44:17-19, 25.
98. Ezekiel 8:14.
99. Revelation 17:5.

Mormo. The word Mormon literally means "Death-Moon" (from *mor*, "death," and *mon*, "Moon"). More generally speaking, Mormon translates as "a follower of the Death-Moon-Goddess Mormo."[100]

The Great Goddess of the Mormons is not simply an arcane image of the Divine Feminine. According to LDS authorities like Daniel H. Ludlow, she is the literal wife of God, a female Supreme Being that Mormons fondly refer to as "Mother in Heaven," or the "Heavenly Mother."

Catholics would not recognize this deity as the Virgin Mary. However, she is identical to the many old Pagan goddesses who served as prototypes for Mary. In fact, the Latter-Day Saints' "Heavenly Mother" is none other than the great universal Pagan Whore-Mother-Goddess, whose existence Mormons infer from a passage in the book of Genesis (1:27),[101] and who was long variously known across the ancient world by a myriad of names, though primarily as Aphrodite, "Porne," the "Mother of All Harlots."

THE TRUE ORIGINS & MEANING OF MARRIAGE
Yes, the modern worship of the Great Whore is never far from us. Not even when we marry.

Our modern English word marriage comes from the ancient phrase, "Mari Tare," meaning "union under the sacred auspices of the Whore-Mother-Goddess Mari."

Our word-phrase "Holy Matrimony" has similar origins. Holy derives from the word *hol*, or as we now spell it, hole, the dark cave-like symbol of Goddess' sacred Yoni (recall that the ancient Semitic word for hole or cave is *hor* or *whore*).

The word Hell is related to *hol* as well: one of Goddess' ancient Germanic names is Hol, Hel, or Hell ("One Who Hides"), the name given to the dark Christian Underworld by anti-Goddess Christian males. (Note: Christian mythographers intentionally located Hell in the midst of the body of Goddess; that is, at the center of the Earth.)

---

100. In this guise Mormo is thus indistinguishable from other Underworld-Goddesses, such as the Hindus' Kali-Ma, whose name means "Dark Mother."
101. Naturally, the non-Bible based Mormons do not discuss their belief in a Pagan Mother-Goddess in public, just as they do not openly admit to a belief in a "plurality" of other deities, the secret ritual of baptism for the dead (condemned in 1 Corinthians 15:29 by Saint Paul as a Pagan practice), the belief that Jesus and Satan are brothers, the posthumous attainment of self-godhood (in order to rule other planets after earthly death), the belief that the Pagan (Mesoamerican) Serpent-God Quetzalcoatl is the resurrected Jesus, and the continuance of male polygamy after death, among many other unorthodox dogmas.

The word matrimony derives from the words *matri*, meaning "mother" or "earth" (the words material and matter derive from matri) and the word *mon*, meaning "Moon."

The phrase Holy Matrimony then literally means, "Goddess Mother-Moon"; or esoterically, "union under the aegis of the Life-Bearing Sacred Yoni of the Great Earth-Moon-Mother-Goddess, Hol."

We will note here that our modern English word man is a corruption of the Old English word *mon*, meaning "moon," a word that originally meant "female." After the Patriarchal Takeover around 6000 BCE, the word mon or man was stolen from women and applied to males, an act meant to devitalize and devalue the human female.

Eventually, patriarchalists arrogantly transformed the word Man into a term-word meant to denote both the human male *and* the human female—creating such words, for example, as mankind, humanity, and anthropology, the latter literally meaning "the scientific study of Man." (To my knowledge no study has ever been undertaken to find out how men would feel if all humans were referred to as Woman, and the scientific study of humans was called gynopology.)

GODDESS' SACRED DAY
Naturally, with its twenty-eight-day cycle, the Moon is Goddess' sacred celestial sphere. In ancient times the first day of the sacred *seven*-day week (a number based on Goddess' four-week, twenty-eight-day, thirteen-month Lunar Year), was called "Moon's Day," or as we now know it in its corrupted English form, Monday.

Patriarchalists later transferred the first day of the week to the "Sun's Day," or Sunday, the traditional day on which the great male Sun-God was, and is still, worshiped. In the process they arrogantly recast Sunday as the "first day of the week." But Monday, or rather Moon's Day, is still regarded as the first day of the week by Goddess-worshipers around the world.

THE NAMES OF GOD & CHRIST
Known originally as Zeus, Jove, or Jupiter, early Jews and Christians borrowed the archetypal figure of the Pagan Sun-God and appended it to their own myths and theologies.

In Judaism Jove was hebracized, becoming Jahu, Yahi, or Jahveh, or Yhwh (with vowels, Yahweh).

Later, Christians borrowed the all-consonant Hebrew name Yhwh, and combined it (every other letter) with the vowels of Adonai, the name of a pre-Christian Syrian Pagan Savior (in Greece he was known as Adonis). The result was the Pagan-Semitic hybrid name: Yahoweh, Jehovah, Joshua, Jason, or, in its modern corrupted English form, Jesus.

Even the title-name Christ (and thus the word Christianity) derives from the Great Whore-Mother-Goddess. We will recall that Christ, or *Christos,* is a Greek derivation of the old Mesopotamian word *chrs* or *chris*, meaning the "Sun," a word that also gave rise to *chrism*, the "bright" and "shining" oil used in Goddess' christing (anointing) rituals.

THE WHORE-MOTHER AS SUN-GODDESS

Long before the rise of Christianity, the Sun was held to be the daytime aspect of the Whore-Goddess (just as the Moon was her nighttime aspect). Ancient Hindus called the Sun-Goddess Aditi: "she who is clothed with the Sun."

Like all early forms of Goddess, Aditi was portrayed with twelve starchildren (creating the magical, and feminine number of fortune, thirteen), symbolized in the golden tiara of twelve glittering stars that she wore.

To the early Japanese the Sun-Goddess was Omikami Amaterasu; to the early Arabs she was Atthar; the ancient Celts knew her as Sulis; the early Norwegians referred to her as Sol; the ancient Germans called her Sunna; and to the ancient Romans she was Minerva.

The prehistoric origins of the Sun as the Great Whore-Mother become clear when we realize that she was worshiped all across the ancient Indo-European world as Mari, which is why early Tantric Buddhists called their Sun-Goddess Marici.

Early Jewish and Christian mythographers adopted the Hindu Sun-Goddess Aditi and appended her to the figure of the Virgin Mary. To this day a very Pagan-like Mary appears in the New Testament book of Revelation as the "woman clothed with the sun, and the moon under her feet, and upon her head a crown of twelve stars."[102] Here, Mary and her twelve-star tiara represent the pre-Christian Pagan Mother-Whore-Goddess and her Twelve Star-Children, equaling the magic female number, thirteen.

Little wonder that the Virgin Mary appeared to her followers at Fatima, Portugal, for six consecutive months on the *thirteenth* day of each month (May 13, 1917, through October 13, 1917).

---

102. Revelation 12:1.

HOW THE PAGAN SUN-GODDESS BECAME THE CHRISTIAN SON-GOD

When original Christianity (that is, Gnosticism) passed into the hands of patriarchal misogynists, going from a small mystical lunar-solar cult to a large orthodox commercialized religion in the 2nd Century (that is, Catholicism), the word "Sun" began to be spelled "Son."[103]

It was at this time that the reigns of male power were personified in the figure of the great spiritual teacher Jesus, known revealingly in ancient times to Christians as both "the Sun of Righteousness"[104] and the "Son of God."[105] Though as a Christian I believe Jesus to be both the Son of God and a historical person who lived in the 1st Century, the Bible, as well as contemporary writers, clearly show that the Nazarene carpenter was both paganized and apotheosized by early Catholic authorities, an attempt to make Him more palatable to the converting masses of Pagans.

Thus, as late as the 3rd Century, Roman Christians were still openly venerating Jesus as a Pagan solar deity. A Christian mosaic in an ancient Roman tomb under Saint Peter's Basilica from this period, for example, portrays Jesus as the Greek Sun-God Apollo, riding his fiery chariot across the heavens. Apollo's title, Phoebus, means "the Bright One," and so one of Jesus' titles became "the Bright and Morning Star."[106]

---

103. The Indo-European languages have preserved this linguistic alteration. In German, for instance, Sun is still spelled *Sonne*.
104. Malachi 4:2.
105. Mark 1:1.
106. Revelation 22:16. We will note here that biblical writers also referred to Satan as the "Morning Star." In the book of Isaiah, for example, the original Hebrew word *Heylel*, meaning "Morning Star," is translated as the word Lucifer (see 14:12). That both Jesus and the Devil were given the title Morning Star certainly ties in with the Mormon belief that the two are brothers. However, there is a deeper esoteric meaning that is unknown to many people: according to mystics like the Gnostics and the Kabbalists, God and Satan are one and the same; occultically their names are even a reversal of one another. In ancient Rome this idea was articulated in the saying: *Demon est Deus inversus* ("the Devil is God reversed"). While Isaiah 45:7 hints at this truth, we do have definitive biblical evidence: the name Lucifer means "Bringer of Light," while the name Christ means "the Sun." Furthermore, the "Bright and Morning Star" is none other than the planet Venus, named after the ancient Romans' holy celestial harlot, the great and mighty Sex-Goddess Venus, known to the Greeks as Aphrodite. What does all of this mean? For those "who have eyes to see" (i.e., use of the Third Eye), the paths of both Jesus (spirituality) and Satan (materialism) lead to the same goal: enlightenment ("the mind of Christ," as Saint Paul called it), the highest and purest level of consciousness; one that the Great Whore-Goddess and her daughters (prostitutes) promise to those who partake in their pleasures. In the end there are many paths to God/dess. Aphrodite's way is the Tantric Way, the Yada of the Old Testament, the Ginosko of the New Testament.

CHRISTMAS & THE WHORE-GODDESS

Even the Pagan Sun-Goddess' sacred birthday, December 25, was borrowed from the Pagans and given to the historical Jesus.

Long celebrated by the Romans as *Dies Natalis Sol Invictus* ("Rebirth of the Invincible Sun-God"), and held on the final day of the week-long *Saturnalia* winter festival, orthodox Christian priests renamed the Pagan holy day the "Mass of Christ" (or "Christmas") in an attempt to win Pagan Moon-Goddess and Sun-God worshiping converts to the Church.

What was so special about December 25?

This is the general time of the Winter Solstice, when the days begin to grow longer, and the Sun ("Son") appears to be "born again," or "resurrected," as it passes through the astrological version of the Virgin-Whore-Mother-Goddess, the constellation of Virgo (the "Virgin"). Indeed, what is now called Christmas Eve was originally known in ancient Pagan Rome as *Matrum Noctem*, "the Night of the Mother," in honor of the Great Virgin (Virgo) who gives new life to her Divine Sun/Son-God each year at the Winter Solstice.

With its gift-giving, holly boughs, pine trees, mistletoe, Yule logs, colorful decorations, feasting, drinking, candles, incense, caroling, prayers, and general merriment (all derive from the ancient worship of Goddess), Christmas is one of the more overtly Pagan of Christianity's holy days.

This is why, in fact, Eastern Churches did not accept the idea of Christmas until the late 4th Century, while the Jerusalem Church rejected it until the 7th Century. Many modern Christian denominations and sects, from the 17th-Century Puritans to some 21st-Century Protestant Churches, continue to ban, or at least discourage, the celebration of Christmas for just these reasons.[107]

THE PATRIARCHALIZATION PROCESS

Through the assimilation of these Pagan ideas and practices, early Christian authorities managed to transform the Great Whore-Mother Mari, her custom of sacred prostitution, and her holy bonding ritual, "Mari Tare," into patriarchal symbols and practices.

As a result, most women today continue to not only take their husband's first and last names after marriage, but allow their children to be

---

[107]. As mentioned, for a detailed discussion on the paganization of Jesus and the christianization of the Winter Solstice, see my book *Christmas Before Christianity: How the Birthday of the "Sun" Became the Birthday of the "Son."*

given the father's last name as well. Even a woman's so-called "maiden-name" is derived from a male: her father.

This androcentric custom (called patronymicism) is the opposite of that found in the Goddess world of prehistoric and ancient times, when men took their wives' names and women named their children after themselves, a practice (called matronymicism) well documented in the remains of Neolithic settlements and in ancient historical records.[108]

---

108. A modern vestige of ancient matronymicism can still be found in Scandinavia, where it is not uncommon to find surnames such as Friddasdottir ("Frida's daughter"). There are also such examples as Bengtsdotter ("Benedict's daughter"), Jansdotter ("John's daughter"), Eriksdottir ("Eric's daughter"), and Halfdansdotter ("Half Dane's daughter").

10
PROSTITUTION: THE NOBLE HERITAGE

PATRIARCHAL MARRIAGE IS SANCTIONED PROSTITUTION

BY institutionalizing Goddess' sacred ritual of prostitution under the Goddess word "marriage," our patriarchal Judeo-Christian-based society thus continues to keep Aphrodite's Trade alive.

As noted earlier, all American states have laws that require married men to financially support their wives, while at the same time requiring married women to provide sex for their husbands.

There is only one word for this type of relationship form, and it is prostitution, which is exactly how Webster, and most contemporary sexologists and feminists, define it.

Even in countries where polygyny (a man having multiple wives simultaneously) is practiced, we find the same established custom of "marriage-as-institutionalized prostitution," revealing that the oldest profession in the world has not been exterminated. We can say quite factually, primatologically at least, that it has merely been renamed and sanctioned under the patriarchal catch-phrase "monogamous marriage."

Does this make monogamous marriage an immoral institution? Hardly. This is only to point out that at its roots monogamous marriage is not a romantic relationship, as our society continues to maintain. It is an evolutionarily designed business partnership, one that not only brings comfort, stability, security, and enjoyment to those involved, but which also increases one's chance of survival, the very reason prostitutionary relationships arose among our prehistoric ancestors to begin with.

HOROLOGY & THE SEX-WORKER PROFESSION

It is interesting to note that the modern science of measuring time is still called horology by modern clock-makers, time-keepers, and other horologers.

Few realize, however, that the name originally honored the ancient Whore-Mother-Goddess (Hor), the Sacred Whore Wisdom (attaining spiritual enlightenment through sex), the ancient dancing temple hors (Goddess' priestesses), and all female sex workers in general (in modern times these would include escorts, street-walkers, dominatrices, adult film actors, phone sex operators, dancers, etc.).

THE WHORE-MOTHER'S CONNECTION TO TIME, INTELLIGENCE, LIFE, WOMEN, & EARTH

The importance of the Whore-Mother and her relationship with not only time, but with many other aspects of life, can be traced etymologically through language.

All of the following words, for example, are derived (directly or indirectly) from the ancient Indo-European morphemes or root-words *ma*, *mo*, *mu*, or *me*, meaning "woman" or "mother": mammal, mammary, man, Marie, Maria, Marian, marriage, Mary, mate, material, maternal, math, matriarch, matrimony, matrix, matter, mature, matutinal, maun, measure, memory, men, menarche, menhir, menopause, menorah, menses, menstrual, menstruation, mental, meridian, mermaid, merry, metabolic, metal, metallurgy, metamorphosis, meteor, meteorite, meteorology, meter, metestrus, metric, metrology, metropolitan, mind, mom, monarch, monarchy, monastery, Monday, monetary, money, monogamy, monolith, *mons veneris*, month, Moon, moor, morbid, morganatic, Mormon, morning, mortal, mortuary, mother, mound, mount, mountain, mum, murder, murky, muse, and myrrh.

The whole history of women and their many contributions to the world, from language and writing to politics and religion, could be written from an examination of these few words alone.

PROSTITUTION & THE SURVIVAL OF HOMO SAPIENS

Today's sex workers have a truly long and noble heritage that is ensconced in the eternal worship of the Great Mother as both Whore and Madonna; a heritage that began millions of years ago among our distant primate ancestors; one that helped our particular hominid species survive while others perished.

And indeed, many did.

Among the extinct humans of the Genus *Homo* are: *Homo rudolfensis*, *Homo habilis*, *Homo georgicus*, *Homo ergaster*, *Homo erectus*, *Homo antecessor*, *Homo heidelbergensis*, *Homo neanderthalensis*, *Homo floresiensis*, and *Homo sapiens idaltu*. Of these many fellow members in our family tree, we alone, *Homo sapiens sapiens*, managed to endure, outlasting even the tough and astute Neanderthal (whose brain, in some cases, was larger than ours).

We owe our incredible and unlikely survival, in great part, to Aphrodite's Trade, and the prostitution gene that created it, for we would not be here now if it had not been for the prostitutionary relationships of prehistoric peoples, nor would monogamous marriage be able to function today if it were not itself a form of prostitution. For while long-term monogamy is unnatural to humans,[109] short-term monogamy (that is, serial polygamy)—along with its prostitutionary quality—is firmly grounded in our biological primate past.

THE LIGHT OF KNOWLEDGE

Let us then not allow those individuals whose minds are shackled by ignorance, patriarchal phobias, religious prejudice, and misogynistic attitudes, to pervert that heritage.

Just as lies can be taught and accepted, they can also be unlearned and rejected. In place of these stygian falsehoods we must illuminate the world, teaching others the truth about prostitution. For by filling the mind with the light of knowledge, we may drive out the darkness of intolerance, fear, and bigotry.

APHRODITE'S DAUGHTERS

Lastly, let us make one fact perfectly clear: all female sex workers and sex care providers are descended from a great and regal tradition in which a woman was once regarded as an earthly embodiment of the first Supreme Being, Goddess herself, an eternal image who is, at the same time, both deeply spiritual *and* intensely sexual. Hence, one of the many positive nicknames for prostitutes: Aphrodite's Daughters.

Yes, it is true that this respectful tradition has largely disappeared today. Can it be resuscitated? The answer is yes. The question is how?

---

[109]. By this I do not mean to infer that long-term, or even lifelong, monogamy is either impossible or undesirable. I am saying that because it is not biologically hardwired into us, it is very difficult for most people. Indeed, this is why as a religious and societal ideal, not to mention as an actual practice, lifetime monogamy (sex with only one person for life) is found in so few societies. And this is also why most human beings never come close to achieving it. If it *were* biologically natural to us, the statistics would be the opposite: most people would easily form and maintain lifelong monogamous relationships, while only a tiny minority would fail.

With the individual female prostitute, who must begin looking at herself as one who fulfills an all-important role in human society; an honored role; an aristocratic role; a biological role; a medical role; a therapeutic role; even a spiritual role.

In addition, attorneys sympathetic to the sex work industry will need to work to change both thinking and laws until prostitution is finally sanctioned and decriminalized.

NURSES OF THE BODY & SOUL

Despite the commercialized, debased, and wholly secular nature of contemporary Western prostitution, female whores still truly remain the matriarchal "Daughters of Goddess" (as opposed to the patriarchal "Sons of God"), true offspring of the Universal Sex- and Love-Goddess Aphrodite, who helps men achieve spiritual enlightenment (known variously as Nirvana, Christ, Christ Consciousness, the Kingdom of God, the Crown [Chakra], Samadhi, the Way, Yada, Ginosko, and Cosmic Consciousness) via the Tantric Path.

And so whores are the nurses of both the body and soul. Indeed, it is their willingness to give (whether for financial gain or pleasure) what so many others withhold that sets prostitutes apart from, and above, all other women.

THE WOMEN OF APHRODITE'S TRADE

Contrary to popular opinion, prostitutes do not try to deceive. They merely see the world for what it is; men for who they are; commerce for what it is.

Yet for this honesty they are demonized and locked away in prisons by both the religious and atheists alike; often even by the very men who pay them for their time and services *and* punish them later.[110]

Prostitutes are angels of mercy, yet they are portrayed as devils of cruelty for their love of money and sex.

They are wise, but are made to look stupid.
They are worldly, but are portrayed as naive.
They are compassionate, but are described as heartless.
They are beautiful, but are made to look ugly.
They are winners in a world of fierce competitiveness, but are depicted as losers.

---

110. As any prostitute will tell you, a healthy percentage of her clientele is comprised of politicians, judges, and police officers—most of them married.

They are financially shrewd, but are depicted as greedy.

They have saved many a marriage, but are called home wreckers.

They have healed many a broken heart, but for their effort they have their own hearts broken in return by an uninformed, unfeeling world.

They have saved many souls from the jaws of Hell, but are banished there themselves by "God-loving" believers.

Prostitutes make hypocrites of society, and in return society makes them criminals.

All of this is why, in defending the royal profession of Sacred Whoredom and Harlotry against the sanctimonious declarations of Medieval Catholicism, the 15th-Century Italian philosopher Lorenzo Valla had this to say about the women who work in Aphrodite's Trade:

> Whores and prostitutes deserve more from the human race than do nuns with all of their chastity and virginity!

APPENDIX A

MYTHS ABOUT DECRIMINALIZING PROSTITUTION

MYTH: It's an immoral profession. So decriminalizing it would be promoting immorality.
FACT: Some of the world's greatest minds, among them philosophers, scholars, theologians, politicians, and scientists, have supported decriminalization. Many religious authorities throughout history have approved of prostitution as well, including a number of popes. Even Jesus did not condemn it. Thus, whether prostitution is immoral or not is a subjective opinion. Also, do we really want the government regulating morality? What if a group campaigns, and finally succeeds, at making something illegal that you consider moral? Where does it end? The Founding Fathers gave the U.S. (Federal) Government only two true powers: guarantee to the states of a republican form of government and the protection of her citizens from foreign invasion and domestic violence.[111] Beyond this everything else is unconstitutional and an intrusion upon the rights of the American people (see the Tenth Amendment). Certainly Founders like Thomas Jefferson, what we would today call a libertarian, would have never sanctioned the criminalization of prostitution. To our detriment and peril we have veered far away from the original Constitution and the intentions of the Founding Fathers.

MYTH: There would be an explosion of prostitution everywhere, with millions of girls and women selling their bodies for money.
FACT: Millions of girls and women worldwide are already selling their bodies for money. Decriminalizing the profession would not change this. What it would do is change them from criminals to law abiding citizens. This would immediately bring a host of benefits, among them: making life better and safer for prostitutes, easing up the court and penal system, and lowering the cost to the tax payer—whose personal income now goes to

---

111. See Article 4, Section 4, of the U.S. Constitution. Known as the "Guarantee Clause," it is attributed to Founding Father James Madison.

pursuing, entrapping, arresting, lawyering, convicting, jailing, feeding, clothing, housing, and rehabilitating innocent "criminals."

MYTH: Decriminalization would create a less safe and a less stable society.
FACT: Prostitution being a crime is what creates an unsafe and an unstable society. Remember Prohibition?

MYTH: There would be a huge increase in the rates of sexually transmitted diseases (STDs).
FACT: The vast majority of female prostitutes are extremely cautious and knowledgeable when it comes to STDs, far more, in fact, than the average woman. This would not change with decriminalization. The reality is that prostitutes are the givers and receivers of very few diseases: scientific studies conducted by the Center for Disease Control show that in the U.S. prostitutes are only responsible for 3 to 5 percent of all STDs. At least 75 percent of all STDs derive from high school and college students, while the remaining 20 percent or so result from non-commercial interactions, such as one-night stands. One is *least* likely then to contract an STD from a prostitute, and is *most* likely to contract one from a teenager or college student.

MYTH: Millions of men would feel free to begin cheating.
FACT: Men who are prone to infidelity will cheat whether prostitution is decriminalized or not. Likewise, men who are not prone to unfaithfulness will not be tempted to do so just because a law is altered. In short, there will always be the type of man who cheats no matter what. One must also consider the findings of numerous polls: if forced to choose between a prostitute and an affair, the vast majority of wives would prefer that their husbands occasionally visit the former rather than get both sexually *and* emotionally involved with another woman.[112]

MYTH: Decriminalizing prostitution would destroy our Christian society.
FACT: Things that actually hurt and even kill people are perfectly legal, such as cigarettes, alcohol, and a high fat diet. Yet society has not crumbled

---

112. For men, prostitutes provide the benefit of fast, uncomplicated, no-strings-attached sex. Whether society likes to admit it or not, this particular aspect of prostitution also benefits the wives and families of such men. In fact, the vast majority of marriages are "wrecked," not by husbands visiting prostitutes, but by husbands getting involved in long, drawn out, emotionally charged affairs with non-prostitute women.

and disappeared as a result. And prostitution is certainly no threat to the Christian Church, which once supported the profession and even owned and operated brothels. As Saint Augustine pointed out nearly 2,000 years ago, permitting prostitution would actually help strengthen society *and* Christianity by acting as a safety valve that siphons off the excess pressure caused by monogamous marriage, an institution for which we humans are not biologically adapted.

MYTH: Decriminalization would lure untold numbers of females into the trade who would not have gone into it otherwise.
FACT: Those who are really interested in prostitution are already in the business.

MYTH: It would destroy the idea of marriage.
FACT: Even with prostitution being illegal, 60 percent of marriages in the U.S. end in divorce.[113] It is the belief of some authorities that decriminalized prostitution would have saved many of these unions. There are also differing opinions as to what constitutes a marriage. For example, radical feminists often define monogamous marriage as simply legalized prostitution. According to this view, millions of women already enjoy the benefits of lawful harlotry: wives. The truth of the matter is that prostitution is the scaffolding on which monogamous marriage is built. Therefore, as some of the early Christian Fathers observed, far from destroying marriage, prostitution actually supports and maintains it—both inside and outside the institution.

MYTH: Prostitution is sexual slavery. To decriminalize it would be to encourage the enslavement and rape of women.
FACT: This, the battle cry of both religious fundamentalists and radical feminists, is an egregious error and reveals a voluminous dearth of familiarity with Aphrodite's Trade. Prostitution can be broken into two basic types: voluntary and involuntary. In no way, shape, or form do decriminalization proponents condone involuntary sex work, which violates every known civil, social, moral, ethical, and religious law. As for voluntary prostitution, since it occurs between consenting adults, we believe that under the Constitution the government has no right to meddle. We will

---

113. Hollywood couples and teens have even higher divorce rates.

state here that many people support decriminalization who do not necessarily like or approve of prostitution itself. These are two different issues, the former a legal and constitutional matter, the latter a personal and subjective one.

MYTH: If we decriminalize prostitution, why not drugs and gambling?
FACT: Exactly.

MYTH: Selling sex for money is disgusting and should not be encouraged.
FACT: Baseball pitchers and football quarterbacks sell their arms for money. Soccer players and long-distance runners sell their legs for money. Surrogate mothers sell their wombs for money. Models sell nearly every part of their bodies for money. Adult film actors are even paid to have sex on screen. Why then should an ordinary woman not be able to sell her sexual services for money? Why is it alright to sell a uterus, and literally every other part of a woman's body, but not a vagina? Why is it okay to pay a woman to have sex in public (as in an adult film), but it is not okay to pay this same woman to have sex in private (as in prostitution)? In other words, why is it legal for a woman to have sex with a man for the purpose of business, but it is illegal for her to have sex with him for the purpose of pleasure? It is because we are still steeped in a male-dominant, puritanical culture that does not equate sex with enjoyment and that wants to control the sexuality of women.[114]

MYTH: Allowing prostitution to become a legitimate occupation is not rational.
FACT: Allowing prostitution to remain an illegitimate occupation is not rational. Consider this: if a man takes a woman out to a restaurant and pays for her dinner, then buys her a gift and takes her to movie, then takes her home and has sex with her, neither one has broken any law, even though they have clearly traded money for sex. However, if this same man skips dinner, the gift, and the movie, and just pays the woman directly for sex, both are now criminals. And again, to re-emphasize: when a man and woman are paid to have sex in front of a camera (as in adult films), they are

---

114. Prostitutes want it known that not all "transactions" include sexual intercourse. Typically most modern men who visit prostitutes, as did their ancient counterparts, just want a moment to luxuriate in the company of a female. Why? They find it re-energizing, as men lack the Shaktic energy (the procreative life-force) possessed by women.

law-abiding citizens. In fact, they can have any kind of sex they like with as many people as they like without breaking a single law. But if this same couple even agrees to exchange money for sex in the privacy of one of their own homes, they are outlaws.

MYTH: Decriminalizing prostitution would put the lives and welfare of prostitutes in jeopardy.
FACT: The complete opposite is true. In fact, in New Zealand, where all sex work (including prostitution) was wisely decriminalized in 2003, one study found that decriminalization has had almost nothing but positive effects concerning the safety and health of prostitutes. In truth, most individuals who are against decriminalization only take the position above because they do not approve of prostitution, completely disregarding the compassionate ideas, logical reasoning, bold facts, and biological truths laid out in this book. It is *these* very people—that is, those who keep Aphrodite's Trade illegal—who put the well-being of prostitutes at risk.

MYTH: The push to decriminalize prostitution is a right-wing conspiracy, advocated by conservatives who want to force their outdated values on everyone else.
FACT: Not true. Liberal Democrat Dr. Joycelyn Elders, U.S. Surgeon General under liberal democratic President Bill Clinton, supports the decriminalization of prostitution.

MYTH: The push to decriminalize prostitution is a left-wing conspiracy, advocated by liberals hell-bent on ruining American society.
FACT: Wrong. The late conservative libertarian William F. Buckley, Jr., founder of the conservative magazine *The National Review*, was just one of many on the right who support the idea of decriminalizing prostitution.

APPENDIX B

Positive & Negative Synonyms Used for the Word Prostitute

Note that many of these are actual Goddess names, some from the Bible

adultress
Aphrodite's daughter
banshee
B-girl
bawd
bedmate
beldame
best girl
betrayer
bimbo
bitch
broad
call girl
camp follower
Casanova (male)
chatelaine
cheater
chippy
Circe
concubine
courtesan
daughter of Aphrodite
daughter of joy
deceiver
Delilah
demimondaine
Don Juan (male)
doxy
dragon

easy make
enchantress
escort
fallen angel
fallen woman
fancy woman
fille de joie
fishwife
floozy
Fury
gigolo (male)
Gorgon
hag
harlot
harpy
harridan
hooker
hustler
hussy
jade
Jezebel
lady of the evening
light o' love
loose woman
madam
maenad
Magdalene
Medusa
mistress

moll
nag
nixie
nymphomaniac
ogress
painted woman
paramour
pervert
pickup
piece of tail
priestess
pro
procuress
putain
seducer
serpent
shack job
shrew
siren
slattern
sloven
slut
snake
sorceress
streetwalker
strumpet
tart
temptress
tramp
trollop
trull
V-girl
virago
vixen
wanton
wench
whore
witch
woman of the streets

working girl

APPENDIX C

Words & Phrases Used for the Profession or Act of Prostitution

Aphrodite's trade (coined by the author)
carry on
concubinage
cuckoldry
harlotry
horizontal refreshment (American Civil War)
on the game
pander
pandering
sleep around
venery
wenching
whoring

APPENDIX D

Words & Phrases Used for a House of Prostitution

bagnio
bawdyhouse
bordello
brothel
call house
cathouse
combat zone
den of iniquity
den of vice
house of assignation
house of ill fame
house of ill pleasure
house of ill repute
house of shame
house with red doors
joy house
red-light district
whorehouse

APPENDIX E

Words Used in the Past in Relationship to the Word Prostitute

adoration
adulation
advisor
amazing
angel
angelic
anoint
anointed
apotheosis
atonement
beauty
bless
blessing
celebration
celestial
champion
charmer
coach
confidence
Cytherean
deification
deipotent
devotion
dignity
distinction
diva
divine
divinity
dryad
educator
elevation

enlightener
enlightenment
esteem
exaltation
exemplar
fairy
faith
fame
glory
goddess
grace
greatness
guide
hallowed
heaven
heavenly
heroine
high standing
holiness
holy
homage
honor
idolize
immortalization
instructor
laud
laurel
lionization
majesty
mentor
mercy

merciful
mistress
mother
mothering
naiad
Nirvana
nurse
nurturer
nurturing
nymph
omnipotent
popularity
praise
preceptor
prestige
priestess
pure
purity
recognition
redemption
religion
religious
religious teacher
renown
repute
respect
revere
reverence
reverent
sacred
sacrosanct
sage
saint
saintly
sanctified
sanctity
seraphic
sex symbol
sister

spirit
spiritual
spirituality
sprite
star
sylph
sylphic
teacher
trainer
tribute
tutor
unearthly
veneration
victory
wisdom
wise
worship

APPENDIX F

Words Used Today in Relationship to the Word Prostitute

abhor
abnormal
abuse
addict
adultery
animal
atheism
atheist
aversion
befoul
bitch
blaspheme
blemish
buggery
cheapen
contamination
corruption
cruel
cruelty
curse
damnation
debasement
debauchery
deceiver
defile
degradation
demean
demoralize
denunciation
depravity
depredation

derision
desecration
despoil
detestation
devalue
Devil
devil worshiper
dirt
dirty
disapproval
disgrace
disgust
dishonor
disrespect
dissipation
druggie
enchantress
execration
exploitation
evil
fakery
felon
femme fatale
filth
hatred
home wrecker
humiliation
loathsome
loser
loss
lost

mess up
molestation
outrage
perversion
pervert
pity
pollution
profane
promiscuous
revile
ruination
sacrilege
Satan
satanic
scorn
screw up
seductress
sexpot
shame
sick
sickness
sin
sinner
slut
slutty
sodomy
sodomite
squander
stigma
stupidity
tainted
temptress
trash
ugly
ugliness
vamp
vice
violate
vitiation

waste
wench
witch
wrong

APPENDIX G

World Charter For Prostitutes' Rights

From the International Committee for
Prostitutes' Rights (ICPR), Amsterdam, 1985

Cited from the book *A Vindication of the Rights of Whores*,
with the kind permission of the author, Gail Pheterson

LAWS

Decriminalize all aspects of adult prostitution resulting from individual decision.

Decriminalize prostitution and regulate third parties according to standard business codes. It must be noted that existing standard business codes allow abuse of prostitutes. Therefore special clauses must be included to prevent the abuse and stigmatization of prostitutes (self-employed and others).

Enforce criminal laws against fraud, coercion, violence, child sexual abuse, child labor, rape, racism everywhere and across national boundaries, whether or not in the context of prostitution.

Eradicate laws that can be interpreted to deny freedom of association, or freedom to travel, to prostitutes within and between countries. Prostitutes have rights to a private life.

HUMAN RIGHTS

Guarantee prostitutes all human rights and civil liberties, including the freedom of speech, travel, immigration, work, marriage, and motherhood and the right to unemployment insurance, health insurance and housing.

Grant asylum to anyone denied human rights on the basis of a "crime of status," be it prostitution or homosexuality.

WORKING CONDITIONS

There should be no law which implies systematic zoning of prostitution. Prostitutes should have the freedom to choose their place of work and residence. It is essential that prostitutes can provide their services under the conditions that are absolutely determined by themselves and no one else.

There should be a committee to insure the protection of the rights of the prostitutes and to whom prostitutes can address their complaints. This committee must be comprised of prostitutes and other professionals like lawyers and supporters.

There should be no law discriminating against prostitutes associating and working collectively in order to acquire a high degree of personal security.

HEALTH

All women and men should be educated to periodical health screening for sexually transmitted diseases. Since health checks have historically been used to control and stigmatize prostitutes, and since adult prostitutes are generally even more aware of sexual health than others, mandatory checks for prostitutes are unacceptable unless they are mandatory for all sexually active people.

SERVICES

Employment, counseling, legal, and housing services for runaway children should be funded in order to prevent child prostitution and to promote child well-being and opportunity.

Prostitutes must have the same social benefits as all other citizens according to the different regulations in different countries.

Shelters and services for working prostitutes and re-training programs for prostitutes wishing to leave the life should be funded.

TAXES

No special taxes should be levied on prostitutes or prostitute businesses.

Prostitutes should pay regular taxes on the same basis as other independent contractors and employees, and should receive the same benefits.

PUBLIC OPINION

Support educational programs to change social attitudes which stigmatize and discriminate against prostitutes and ex-prostitutes of any race, gender or nationality.

Develop educational programs which help the public to understand that the customer plays a crucial role in the prostitution phenomenon, this role being generally ignored. The customer, like the prostitute, should not, however, be criminalized or condemned on a moral basis.

We are in solidarity with workers in the sex industry.

ORGANIZATION

Organizations of prostitutes and ex-prostitutes should be supported to further implementation of the above charter.

APPENDIX H

Human Taxonomy

How humans beings are scientifically classified on the family tree of life

KINGDOM: *Animalia* (living organisms)
Subkingdom: *Metazoa* (multicellular animals)

PHYLUM: *Chordata* (animals with spinal chords)
Subphylum: *Vertebrata* (backbone is a simple undivided notochord)
Superclass: *Tetrapoda* (animals with four legs)

CLASS: *Mammalia* (animals with sweat glands, hair, milk production, middle ear bones, and a neocortex)
Subclass: *Theria* (give birth to live young)
Infraclass: *Eutheria* (mammals who nourish the fetus with a placenta)

ORDER: *Primates* (apes—which includes humans, monkeys, and lemurs)
Suborder: *Haplorrhini* (the dry-nosed primates)
Infraorder: *Simiiformes*, formerly *Anthropoidea* (primates with a well-developed brain, upright stance, and no tail)
Parvorder: *Catarrhini* (having narrow, downward-pointing noses; also flat fingernails)

SUPERFAMILY: *Hominoidea* (includes three groups: the human great ape, or *Hominidae*; the nonhuman great apes, or *Pongidae*, that is chimpanzees, gorillas, and orangutans; and the lesser apes, or *Hylobatidae*, that is gibbons and their relatives)

Family: *Hominidae* (the great apes, which includes humans, chimpanzees, gorillas, and orangutans)

Subfamily: *Homininae* (humans, chimpanzees, and gorillas)

Tribe: *Hominini* (humans, chimpanzees, and their extinct ancestors)

Subtribe: *Hominina* (humans only, and their close extinct relatives; currently this would include not only *Homo*, but also *Australopithecus*, *Paranthropus*, *Sahelanthropus*, *Orrorin*, *Ardipithecus*, and *Kenyanthropus*)

GENUS: *Homo* (Latin for "man," *Homo* includes modern humans and their close relatives)

SPECIES: *sapiens* (modern humans only; note: all except we ourselves are now extinct)

Subspecies: *sapiens* (living modern humans only)

Full scientific name: *Homo sapiens sapiens* ("wise wise man")

Be Nice to Sex Workers

Treat them the way you'd want to be treated

BIBLIOGRAPHY

Adler, Margot. *Drawing Down the Moon*. Boston, MA: Beacon Press, 1981.
Agha-Jaffar, Tamara. *Women and Goddesses in Myth and Sacred Text*. New York, NY: Longman, 2004.
Agustín, Laura María. *Sex at the Margins: Migration, Labour Markets and the Rescue Industry*. London, UK: Zed Books, 2007.
Albert, Alexa. *Brothel: Mustang Ranch and Its Women*. New York, NY: Ballantine, 2001.
Albright, William Powell. *Yahweh and the Gods of Canaan*. New York, NY: Doubleday, 1968.
Allen, Paula Gunn. *The Sacred Hoop: Recovering the Feminine in American Indian Traditions*. Boston, MA: Beacon Press, 1986.
Allison, Dale C., Jr. *Resurrecting Jesus: The Earliest Christian Tradition and Its Interpreters*. New York, NY: T and T Clark, 2005.
Almodovar, Norma Jean. *Cop to Call Girl*. New York, NY: Avon, 1994.
———. "For Their Own Good: The Results of the Prostitution Laws as Enforced by Cops, Politicians and Judges." *Hastings Women's Law Journal*. Vol. 10, Number 1, Winter 1999 (University of California, Hastings College of the Law), pp. 119-133.
———. "Porn Stars, Radical Feminists, Cops, and Outlaw Whores: The Battle Between Feminist Theory and Reality, Free Speech, and Free Spirits." *Prostitution and Pornography: Philosophical Debate About the Sex Industry* (Jessica Spector, ed.). Stanford, CA: Stanford University Press, 2006, pp. 149-174.
———. *Cops, Hos, Preachers and Politicos: Commercial $ex $candals in America*. Unpublished manuscript.
Anderson, Ross. *Understanding the Book of Mormon: A Quick Christian Guide to the Mormon Holy Book*. Grand Rapids, MI: Zondervan, 2009.
Andrews, Ted. *The Occult Christ: Angelic Mysteries, Seasonal Rituals, and the Divine Feminine*. St. Paul, MN: Llewellyn, 1993.
Angus, Samuel. *The Mystery-Religions and Christianity: A Study of the Religious Background of Early Christianity*. 1925. New York, NY: Citadel Press, 1966 ed.
Anthony, David W., and Jennifer Y. Chi (eds.). *The Lost World of Old Europe: The Danube Valley, 5000-3500 BC*. Princeton, NJ: Princeton University Press, 2009.
Ardrey, Robert. *African Genesis*. 1961. New York, NY: Dell, 1972 ed.
———. *The Territorial Imperative*. 1966. New York, NY: Delta, 1968 ed.
Armstrong, Herbert W., Keith W. Stump, and John Halford. *The Plain Truth About Christmas*. 1952. Pasadena, CA: Worldwide Church of God, 1986 ed.
Armstrong, Karen. *A History of God: The 4000-Year Quest of Judaism, Christianity and Islam*. New York, NY: Knopf, 1993.
Ashe, Geoffrey. *The Virgin: Mary's Cult and the Re-emergence of the Goddess*. 1976. London, UK: Arkana, 1988 ed.
———. *Dawn Behind the Dawn: A Search for the Earthly Paradise*. New York, NY: Henry Holt, 1992.
Atkins, Gaius Glenn, and Charles Samuel Braden. *Procession of the Gods*. 1930. New York, NY: Harper and Brothers Publishers, 1936 ed.

Attwater, Donald. *The Penguin Dictionary of Saints*. 1965. Harmondsworth, UK: Penguin, 1983 ed.
Avalon, Arthur. *Shakti and Shakta*. New York, NY: Dover, 1978.
Ayto, John. *Dictionary of Word Origins*. New York, NY: Arcade, 1990.
Bachofen, Johann Jakob. *Myth, Religion and Mother Right*. Princeton, NJ: Princeton University Press, 1967.
Baigent, Michael. *The Jesus Papers: Exposing the Greatest Cover-Up in History*. San Francisco, CA: Harper San Francisco, 2006.
Baigent, Michael, and Richard Leigh. *The Dead Sea Scrolls Deception*. 1991. New York, NY: Touchstone, 1993 ed.
Baigent, Michael, Richard Leigh, and Henry Lincoln. *Holy Blood, Holy Grail*. 1982. New York, NY: Dell, 1983. ed.
——. *The Messianic Legacy*. New York, NY: Dell, 1986.
Barash, David P., and Judith Eve Lipton. *The Myth of Monogamy: Fidelity and Infidelity in Animals and People*. New York, NY: Henry Holt, 2001.
Baring, Anne, and Jules Cashford. *The Myth of the Goddess: Evolution of an Image*. 1991. Harmondsworth, UK: Arkana, 1993 ed.
Baring-Gould, Sabine. *Curious Myths of the Middle Ages*. New York, NY: University Books, 1967.
Barnstone, Willis (ed.). *The Other Bible: Ancient Esoteric Texts*. New York, NY: Harper and Row, 1984.
Baroja, Julio Caro. *The World of Witches*. Chicago, IL: University of Chicago Press, 1965.
Barraclough, Geoffrey, and Norman Stone (eds.). *The Times Atlas of World History*. 1978. Maplewood, NJ: Hammond, 1989 ed.
Baumgartner, Anne S. *A Comprehensive Dictionary of the Gods: From Abaasy to Zvoruna*. New York, NY: University Books, 1984.
Bauvel, Robert, and Adrian Gilbert. *The Orion Mystery: Unlocking the Secrets of the Pyramids*. New York, NY: Three Rivers Press, 1995.
Bayley, Harold. *Archaic England: An Essay in Deciphering Prehistory From Megalithic Monuments, Earthworks, Customs, Coins, Place-names, and Faerie Superstitions*. London, UK: Chapman and Hall, 1920.
Beard, Henry, and Christopher Cerf. *The Official Politically Correct Dictionary and Handbook*. New York, NY: Villard Books, 1993.
Bede. *Historia Ecclesiastica Gentis Anglorum (A History of the English Church and People*, Leo Sherley-Price, trans.). C.E. 731. Harmondsworth, UK: Penguin, 1955 (1974 ed.).
Begg, Ean. *The Cult of the Black Virgin*. Harmondsworth, UK: Arkana, 1985.
Bell, Laurie (ed.). *Good Girls/Bad Girls: Feminists and Sex Trade Workers, Face to Face*. Seattle, WA: Seal Press, 1987.
Bell, Robert E. *Women of Classical Mythology: A Biographical Dictionary*. 1991. Oxford, UK: Oxford University Press, 1993 ed.
Bell, Shannon (ed.). *Reading, Writing, and Rewriting the Prostitute Body*. Bloomington, IN: Indiana University Press, 1994.
——. *Whore Carnival*. Brooklyn, NY: Autonomedia, 1995.
Bernstein, Elizabeth. *Temporarily Yours: Intimacy, Authenticity, and the Commerce of Sex*. Chicago, IL: University of Chicago Press, 2007.

Besant, Annie. *Esoteric Christianity or the Lesser Mysteries*. London, UK: Theosophical Publishing Society, 1905.
Best, Robert M. *Noah's Ark and the Ziusudra Epic: Sumerian Origins of the Flood Myth*. Fort Myers, FL: Enlil Press, 1999.
Bhagavad Gita (Juan Mascaró, trans.). 500 BC. Harmondsworth, UK: Penguin, 1962.
Biedermann, Hans. *Dictionary of Symbolism: Cultural Icons and the Meanings Behind Them* (James Hulbert, trans.). 1989. New York, NY: Facts On File, 1992 ed.
Bierlein, John Francis. *Parallel Myths*. New York, NY: Ballantine Wellspring, 1994.
Binder, Pearl. *Magic Symbols of the World*. London, UK: Hamlyn, 1972.
Boardman, John, Jasper Griffin, and Oswyn Murray (eds.). *The Roman World*. 1986. Oxford, UK: Oxford University Press, 1988 ed.
Boates, Karen Scott (ed.). *The Goddess Within*. Philadelphia, PA: Running Press, 1990.
Bostwick, Arthur Elmore (ed.). *Doubleday's Encyclopedia*. 1931. New York, NY: Doubleday, Doran, and Co., 1939 ed.
Bouquet, Alan Coates. *Comparative Religion: A Survey and Comparison of the Great Religions of the World*. London, UK: Penguin, 1942.
Bowden, John. *Archaeology and the Bible*. Austin, TX: American Atheist Press, 1982.
Boyd, Robert, and Joan B. Silk. *How Humans Evolved*. New York, NY: W. W. Norton, 2008.
Branston, Brian. *Gods of the North*. London, UK: Thames and Hudson, 1955.
Bratton, Fred Gladstone. *Myths and Legends of the Ancient Near East: Great Stories of the Sumero-Akkadian, Egyptian, Ugaritic-Canaanite, and Hittite Cultures*. New York, NY: Thomas Y. Crowell, 1970.
Breasted, James Henry. *Ancient Records of Egypt*. 5 vols. Chicago: IL: University of Chicago Press, 1906.
Brewster, Harold Pomeroy. *Saints and Festivals of the Christian Church*. New York, NY: Frederick A. Stokes, 1904.
Bridgwater, William (ed.). *The Columbia-Viking Desk Encyclopedia*. 1953. New York, NY: Viking Press, 1968 ed.
Briffault, Robert Stephen. *The Mothers: The Matriarchal Theory of Social Origins*. 1927. New York, NY: Macmillan, 1931 (single volume, abridged) ed.
Briggs, Katherine. *The Vanishing People: Fairy Lore and Legends*. New York, NY: Pantheon, 1978.
Brownmiller, Susan. *Against Our Will: Men, Women, and Rape*. New York, NY: Fawcett, 1975.
Brownrigg, Ronald. *Who's Who in the New Testament*. 1971. New York, NY: Oxford University Press, 1993 ed.
Bucke, Richard Maurice. *Cosmic Consciousness: A Study in the Evolution of the Human Mind*. 1901. New York, NY: Dutton, 1969 ed.
Budapest, Zsuzsanna Emese. *The Holy Book of Women's Mysteries* (Part 1). 1979. Oakland, CA: Susan B. Anthony Coven No. 1, 1982 ed.
——. *The Holy Book of Women's Mysteries* (Part 2). 1980. Oakland, CA: Susan B. Anthony Coven No. 1, 1982 ed.
Budge, Ernest Alfred Wallis. *Egyptian Magic*. London, UK: Kegan, Paul, Trench, Trübner, and Co., 1901.
——. *Osiris and the Egyptian Resurrection*. Vol. 1. London, UK: Philip Lee Warner, 1911.
——. *Amulets and Talismans*. 1930. New York, NY: Citadel, 1992 ed.

Bulfinch, Thomas. *Bulfinch's Mythology: The Age of Fable, the Age of Chivalry, Legends of Charlemagne.* New York, NY: Thomas Y. Crowell, 1913.

Bullough, Vern, and Bonnie Bullough. *The Subordinate Sex: A History of Attitudes Toward Women.* 1973. Baltimore, MD: Penguin, 1974 ed.

——. *Women and Prostitution: A Social History.* Buffalo, NY: Prometheus, 1987.

Burn, A. R. *The Pelican History of Greece.* 1965. Harmondsworth, UK: Penguin, 1968 ed.

Burne, Jerome (ed.). *Chronicle of the World.* Mount Kisco, NY: Ecam Publications, 1989.

Butler, Trent C. (gen. ed.). *Holman Bible Dictionary.* Nashville, TN: Holman Bible Publishers, 1991.

Caesar, Gaius Julius. *The Conquest of Gaul* [*Gallic War*] (S. A. Handford, trans.). 51 B.C.E. Harmondsworth, UK: Penguin, 1951, 1988 ed.

Calvocoressi, Peter. *Who's Who in the Bible.* 1987. Harmondsworth, UK: Penguin, 1990 ed.

Campanelli, Pauline. *Ancient Ways: Reclaiming Pagan Traditions.* 1991. St. Paul, MN: 1992 ed.

Campbell, Joseph. *The Masks of God: Primitive Mythology.* Vol. 1. 1959. Harmondsworth, UK: Arkana, 1991 ed.

——. *The Masks of God: Oriental Mythology.* Vol. 2. 1962. Harmondsworth, UK: Arkana, 1991 ed.

——. *The Masks of God: Occidental Mythology.* Vol. 3. 1964. Harmondsworth, UK: Arkana, 1991 ed.

——. *The Masks of God: Creative Mythology.* Vol. 4. 1968. Harmondsworth, UK: Arkana, 1991 ed.

——. *Myths to Live By.* New York, NY: Bantam, 1972.

——. *The Power of Myth* (with Bill Moyers). New York, NY: Doubleday, 1988.

——. *Transformations of Myth Through Time.* New York, NY: Harper and Row, 1990.

Camphausen, Rufus C. *The Encyclopedia of Erotic Wisdom.* Rochester, VT: Inner Traditions International, 1991.

Capek, Mary Ellen S. (ed.). *A Woman's Thesaurus: An Index of Language Used to Describe and Locate Information By and About Women.* New York, NY: HarperCollins, 1989.

Carlyon, Richard. *A Guide to the Gods: An Essential Guide to World Mythology.* New York, NY: Quill, 1981.

Carpenter, Edward. *Pagan and Christian Creeds: Their Origin and Meaning*: New York, NY: Blue Ribbon, 1920.

Carson, Anne. *Goddesses & Wise Women: The Literature of Feminist Spirituality, An Annotated Bibliography (1980-1992).* Freedom, CA: Crossing Press, 1992.

Carter, Jesse Benedict. *The Religious Life of Ancient Rome: A Study in the Development of Religious Consciousness, From the Foundation of the City Until the Death of Gregory the Great.* Boston, MA: Houghton Mifflin, 1911.

Cassius, Dio. *The Roman History: The Reign of Augustus* (Ian Scott-Kilvert, trans.). C. 214-226. Harmondsworth, UK: Penguin, 1988.

Cavendish, Richard. *A History of Magic.* 1987. Harmondsworth, UK: Arkana, 1990 ed.

Chapkis, Wendy. *Live Sex Acts: Women Performing Erotic Labor.* New York, NY: Routledge, 1997.

Chetwynd, Tom. *Dictionary of Sacred Myth* ("Language of the Unconscious," Vol. 3). London, UK: Aquarian Press, 1986.

Christie-Murray, David. *A History of Heresy*. Oxford, UK: Oxford University Press, 1976.

Christina, Greta (ed.). *Paying For It: A Guide by Sex Workers For Their Clients*. Oakland, CA: Greenery Press, 2004.

Ciochon, Russell L., and Richard A. Nisbett. *The Primate Anthology: Essays on Primate Behavior, Ecology and Conservation from Natural History*. Upper Saddle River, NJ: Prentice Hall, 1997.

Cirlot, J. E. *A Dictionary of Symbols*. 1962. New York, NY: Philosophical Library, 1983 ed.

Cochran, Gregory, and Henry Harpending. *The 10,000 Year Explosion: How Civilization Accelerated Human Evolution*. New York, NY: Basic Books, 2009.

Collins, Sheila D. *A Different Heaven and Earth: A Feminist Perspective on Religion*. Valley Forge, PA: Judson Press, 1974.

Comay, Joan. *Who's Who in the Old Testament (Together with the Apocrypha)*. 1971. New York, NY: Oxford University Press, 1993 ed.

Condon, R. J. *Our Pagan Christmas*. Austin, TX: American Atheist Press, 1989.

Constable, George (ed.). *Mysteries of the Unknown: Mystic Places*. Richmond, VA: Time-Life, 1987.

Cotterell, Arthur. *A Dictionary of World Mythology*. 1979. New York, NY: Oxford University Press, 1990 ed.

——. *The Macmillan Illustrated Encyclopedia of Myths and Legends*. New York, NY: Macmillan, 1989.

Coulter, Ann. *How to Talk to a Liberal (If You Must): The World According to Ann Coulter*. New York, NY: Three Rivers Press, 2004.

Cross, Frank L., and Elizabeth A. Livingstone. *The Oxford Dictionary of the Christian Church*. 1957. London, UK: Oxford University Press, 1974 ed.

Crossley-Holland, Kevin. *The Norse Myths*. New York, NY: Pantheon, 1980.

Cumont, Franz Valéry Marie. *The Mysteries of Mithra*. New York, NY: Dover, 1956.

——. *Oriental Religions in Roman Paganism*. New York, NY: Dover, 1956.

——. *Astrology and Religion Among the Greeks and Romans*. New York, NY: Dover, 1960.

Curtis, Vesta Sarkhosh. *Persian Myths: The Legendary Past*. Austin, TX: University of Texas Press, 1993.

Dalley, Stephanie (trans.). *Myths From Mesopotamia: Creation, the Flood, Gilgamesh, and Others*. 1989. Oxford, UK: Oxford University Press, 2008 ed.

Daly, Mary. *Beyond God the Father: Toward a Philosophy of Women's Liberation*. Boston, MA: Beacon Press, 1973.

Dank, Barry, and Roberto Refinetti (eds.). *Sex Work and Sex Workers*. Piscataway, NJ: Transaction, 1998.

Darlison, Bill. *The Gospel and the Zodiac: The Secret Truth About Jesus*. New York, NY: Overlook Press, 2008.

Davidson, Gustav. *A Dictionary of Angels*. 1967. New York, NY: The Free Press, 1971 ed.

Davidson, Hilda Roderick Ellis. *Gods and Myths of Northern Europe*. 1964. London, UK: Penguin, 1990 ed.

Davis, Frederick Hadland. *Myths and Legends of Japan.* 1913. Mineola, NY: Dover, 1992 ed.
——. *Pagan Scandinavia.* New York, NY: Frederick A. Praeger, 1967.
——. *Gods and Myths of the Viking Age.* New York, NY: Bell, 1981.
——. *Myths and Symbols in Pagan Europe: Early Scandinavian and Celtic Religions.* Syracuse, NY: Syracuse University Press, 1988.
Davis, John J. *Biblical Numerology: A Basic Study of the Use of Numbers in the Bible.* 1968. Grand Rapids, MI: Baker Book House, 1988 ed.
Day, Sophie. *On the Game: Women and Sex Work.* London, UK: Pluto Press, 2007.
de Beauvoir, Simone. *The Second Sex.* 1952. New York, NY: Vintage, 1989 ed.
Decker, Ed, and Dave Hunt. *The God Makers: A Shocking Expose of What the Mormon Church Really Believes.* Eugene, OR: Harvest House, 1984.
Decker, Ed, and Caryl Matrisciana. *The God Makers II: Startling New Revelations About Modern-Day Mormonism.* Eugene, OR: Harvest House, 1993.
Delacoste, Frederique, and Priscilla Alexander (eds.). *Sex Work: Writings by Women in the Sex Industry.* San Francisco, CA: Cleis Press, 1987.
Delaney, John J. *Pocket Dictionary of Saints.* 1980. New York, NY: Image, 1983 (abridged) ed.
Delehaye, Hippolyte. *The Legends of the Saints: An Introduction to Hagiography.* New York, NY: Fordham University Press, 1962.
Dennis, Rabbi Geoffrey W. *The Encyclopedia of Jewish Myth, Magic and Mysticism.* Woodbury, MN: Llewellyn, 2007.
Derk, Francis H. *A Pocket Guide to the Names of Christ.* 1969. Minneapolis, MN: Bethany House, 1976 ed.
De Rosa, Peter. *Jesus Who Became Christ.* Collins, 1975.
——. *Vicars of Christ: The Dark Side of the Papacy.* New York, NY: Crown, 1988.
——. *Blessed Among Women: The Book of Mary.* Dublin; Ireland: Columba Press, 2005.
de Volney, Constantin François. *The Ruins, or, A Survey of the Revolutions of Empires.* 1791. London, UK: James Watson, 1857 ed.
de Voragine, Jacobus. *The Golden Legend, or Lives of the Saints.* 7 vols. C. 1260. London, UK: J. M. Dent and Co., 1900.
de Waal, Frans. *Chimpanzee Politics: Power and Sex Among Apes.* 1982. Baltimore, MD: John Hopkins University Press, 2000 ed.
——. *Peacemaking Among Primates.* 1989. Cambridge, MA: Harvard University Press, 2002 ed.
——. *Bonobo: The Forgotten Ape.* Berkeley, CA: University of California Press, 1997.
——. *Our Inner Ape: A Leading Primatologist Explains Why We Are, Who We Are.* New York, NY: Riverhead Books, 2005.
Diamond, Jared. *Why Is Sex Fun?: The Evolution of Human Sexuality.* New York, NY: Basic Books, 1997.
Didron, M. *Christian Iconography; or, The History of Christian Art in the Middle Ages.* 2 vols. London, UK: Henry G. Bohn, 1851.
Dione, R. L. *Is God Supernatural?: The 4,000-Year Misunderstanding.* New York, NY: Bantam, 1976.
Ditmore, Melissa Hope (ed.). *Encyclopedia of Prostitution and Sex Work.* 2 vols. Westport, CT: Greenwood Press, 2006.

Doane, Thomas William. *Bible Myths and Their Parallels in Other Religions.* New York, NY: University Books, 1971.

Donahue, Phil. *The Human Animal.* New York, NY: Simon and Schuster, 1988.

Dowley, Tim (ed.). *The History of Christianity.* 1977. Oxford, UK: Lion Publishing, 1990 ed.

Downing, Christine. *The Goddess: Mythological Images of the Feminine.* New York, NY: Crossroads Publishing, 1984.

Dumond, Val. *The Elements of Nonsexist Usage: A Guide to Inclusive Spoken and Written English.* Upper Saddle River, NJ: Prentice Hall, 1990.

Durant, Will. *The Story of Civilization: Volume 1—Our Oriental Heritage.* 1935. New York, NY: Simon and Schuster, 1954 ed.

Eban, Abba. *Heritage: Civilization and the Jews.* New York, NY: Summit, 1984.

Egyptian Book of the Dead, The (E. A. Wallis Budge, trans.). 1895. New York, NY: Dover, 1967 ed.

Ehrlich, Eugene. *Amo, Amas, Amat, and More.* New York, NY: Perennial Library, 1985.

Eisler, Riane. *The Chalice and the Blade: Our History, Our Future.* New York, NY: Perennial Library, 1987.

Elder, Dorothy. *From Metaphysical to Mystical: A Study of the Way.* Denver, CO: Doriel Publishing, 1992.

Eliade, Mircea. *Images and Symbols: Studies in Religious Symbolism.* 1952. Princeton, NJ: Princeton University Press, 1991 ed.

——. *The Sacred and the Profane: The Nature of Religion* (Willard R. Trask, trans.). 1957. San Diego, CA: Harvest, 1959 ed.

——. *A History of Religious Ideas: From Gautama Buddha to the Triumph of Christianity* (Willard R. Trask, trans.). Vol. 2. 1978. Chicago, IL: University of Chicago Press, 1982 ed.

Eliot, Alexander. *The Universal Myths: Heroes, Gods, Tricksters, and Others.* New York, NY: Meridian, 1976.

Elliot, Neil. *Sensuality in Scandinavia.* New York, NY: Weybright and Talley, 1970.

Ellis, Peter Berresford. *A Dictionary of Irish Mythology.* 1987. Oxford, UK: Oxford University Press, 1992 ed.

Elton, Charles Isaac. *Origins of English History.* London, UK: Bernard Quaritch, 1890.

Encyclopedia Britannica: A New Survey of Universal Knowledge. 1768. Chicago, IL/London, UK: Encyclopedia Britannica, 1955 ed.

Eusebius (of Caesarea). *The History of the Church* (G. A. Williamson, trans; Andrew Louth, ed.). Circa C.E. 315-325. Harmondsworth, UK: Penguin, 1965 (1989 ed.).

Evans, Bergen. *Dictionary of Mythology.* 1970. New York, NY: Laurel, 1991 ed.

Evans, Elizabeth Edson. *The Christ Myth: A Study.* New York, NY: Truth Seeker Co., 1900.

Fagan, Brian M. *World Prehistory: A Brief Introduction.* Upper Saddle River, NJ: Prentice Hall, 2007 ed.

Falk, Dean. *Primate Diversity.* New York, NY: W. W. Norton, 2000.

Faludi, Susan. *Backlash: The Undeclared War Against American Women.* New York, NY: Three Rivers Press, 1991.

Farmer, David Hugh. *The Oxford Dictionary of Saints.* 1978. Oxford, UK: Oxford University Press, 1992 ed.

Farr, Kathryn. *Sex Trafficking: The Global Market in Women and Children*. New York, NY: Worth Publishers, 2004.
Farrell, Deborah, and Carole Presser (eds.). *The Herder Symbol Dictionary: Symbols from Art, Archaeology, Mythology, Literature, and Religion* (Boris Matthews, trans.). 1978. Wilmette, IL: Chiron, 1990 ed.
Ferguson, George. *Signs & Symbols in Christian Art*. 1954. London, UK: Oxford University Press, 1975 ed.
Feuerstein, Georg. *Sacred Sexuality: Living the Vision of the Erotic Spirit*. 1992. New York, NY: Tarcher, 1993 ed.
Fideler, David. *Jesus Christ, Sun of God: Ancient Cosmology and Early Christian Symbolism*. Wheaton, IL: Quest, 1993.
Fillmore, Charles, and Theodosia DeWitt Schobert. *Metaphysical Bible Dictionary*. Unity Village, MO: Unity School of Christianity, 1931.
Finegan, Jack. *Light from the Ancient Past: The Archaeological Background of the Hebrew-Christian Religion* (Vol. 1). 1946. Princeton, NJ: Princeton University Press, 1974 ed.
Finger, Ben, Jr. *Concise World History*. New York, NY: Philosophical Library, 1959.
Fischer, Carl. *The Myth and Legend of Greece*. Dayton, OH: George A. Pflaum, 1968.
Fitzgerald, Lisa, Catherine Healy, and Gillian Abel (eds.). *Taking the Crime out of Sex Work: New Zealand Sex Workers' Fight for Decriminalisation*. Bristol, UK: Policy Press, 2010.
Ford, Guy Stanton (ed.-in-chief). *Compton's Pictured Encyclopedia*. 1922. Chicago: F. E. Compton and Co., 1957 ed.
Forrest, M. Isidora. *Offering to Isis: Knowing the Goddess Through Her Sacred Symbols*. St. Paul, MN: Llewellyn, 2005.
Fossey, Dian. *Gorillas in the Mist*. 1983. New York, NY: Mariner Books, 2000 ed.
Fox, Matthew. *The Coming of the Cosmic Christ: The Healing of Mother Earth and the Birth of a Global Renaissance*. New York, NY: Harper and Row, 1988.
Fox, Robin Lane. *Pagans and Christians*. New York, NY: Knopf, 1986.
——. *The Unauthorized Version: Truth and Fiction in the Bible*. New York, NY: Knopf, 1991.
Frazer, Sir James George. *The Golden Bough: A Study in Magic and Religion*. 1922. New York, NY: Collier, 1963 (abridged) ed.
——. *Folklore in the Old Testament*. New York, NY: Tudor Publishing, (abridged) 1923.
Freke, Timothy, and Peter Grandy. *The Jesus Mysteries: Was the Original Jesus a Pagan God?* New York, NY: Three Rivers Press, 1999.
——. *Jesus and the Lost Goddess: The Secret Teachings of the Original Christians*. New York, NY: Three Rivers Press, 2002.
French, Dolores. *Working: My Life As A Prostitute*. Chicago, IL: Trafalgar Square Publishing, 1997.
Freud, Sigmund. *Totem and Taboo*. 1918. New York, NY: Vintage, 1946 ed.
——. *The Future of an Illusion*. 1928. New York, NY: W. W. Norton, 1961 ed.
——. *New Introductory Lectures Psychoanalysis*. Lecture no. 35: "A Philosophy of Life," 1932.
Friedan, Betty. *The Feminine Mystique*. 1963. New York, NY: W. W. Norton, 2001 ed.
Galdikas, Biruté M. F. *Reflections of Eden: My Years with the Orangutans of Borneo*. Boston, MA: Back Bay Books, 1995.

Gantz, Jeffrey (trans.). *Early Irish Myths and Sagas*. 1981. Harmondsworth, UK: Penguin, 1988 ed.

Gaskell, G. A. *Dictionary of All Scriptures and Myths*. 1960. New York, NY: Julian Press, 1973 ed.

Gelling, Peter, and Hilda Ellis Davidson. *The Chariot of the Sun and Other Rites and Symbols of the Northern Bronze Age*. New York, NY: Frederick A. Praeger, 1969.

Gibbons, Ann. *The First Human: The Race to Discover Our Earliest Ancestors*. New York, NY: Anchor, 2007.

Gimbutas, Marija Alseikait. *The Civilization of the Goddess: The World of Old Europe*. New York, NY: HarperCollins, 1991.

———. *The Goddesses and Gods of Old Europe: Myths and Cult Images*. 1974. Berkeley, CA: University of California Press, 1992 ed.

Glyn, Anthony. *The British: Portrait of a People*. New York, NY: G. P. Putnam's Sons, 1970.

Goldenberg, Naomi. *The Changing of the Gods: Feminism and the End of Traditional Religions*. Boston, MA: Beacon Press, 1979.

Goldman, Emma. *The Traffic in Women and Other Essays on Feminism*. Sebastopol, CA: Times Change Press, 1971.

Good, Kay. *In Good Company: The Escort's Guide*. London, UK: Vision, 2006.

Goodall, Jane. *In the Shadow of Man*. 1971. New York, NY: Mariner Books, 2000 ed.

———. *My Life With the Chimpanzees*. New York, NY: Byron Preiss, 1988.

———. *Through a Window: My Thirty Years With the Chimpanzees of Gombe*. 1990. New York, NY: Mariner Books, 2010 ed.

Gordon, Richard Stuart. *The Encyclopedia of Myths and Legends*. 1993. London, UK: Headline, 1994 ed.

Goring, Rosemary (ed.). *Larousse Dictionary of Beliefs and Religions*. 1992. Edinburgh, Scotland: Larousse, 1995 ed.

Graham, Lloyd M. *Deceptions and Myths of the Bible*. 1975. New York, NY: Citadel Press, 1990 ed.

Grant, Michael, and John Hazel. *Who's Who in Classical Mythology*. 1973. New York, NY: Oxford University Press, 1993 ed.

Graves, Kersey. *The World's Sixteen Crucified Saviors, or, Christianity Before Christianity: Containing New, Startling, and Extraordinary Revelations in Religious History, which Disclose the Oriental Origin of All the Doctrines, Principles, Precepts, and Miracles of the Christian New Testament, and Furnishing a Key for Unlocking Many of Its Sacred Mysteries, Besides Comprising the History of Sixteen Heathen Crucified Gods*. Boston, MA: Colby and Rich, 1876.

Graves, Robert. *The Greek Myths*. 1955. Harmondsworth, UK: Penguin, 1992 combined ed.

———. *The White Goddess: A Historical Grammar of Poetic Myth*. 1948. New York, NY: Noonday Press, 1991 ed.

Graves, Robert, and Raphael Patai. *Hebrew Myths: The Book of Genesis*. 1964. New York, NY: Anchor, 1989 ed.

Gray, John. *Near Eastern Mythology: Mesopotamia, Syria, and Palestine*. London, UK: Hamlyn, 1963.

Green, John Richard. *A Short History of the English People* (Vol. 1). London, UK: Macmillan and Co., 1892.

Greenberg, Gary. *The Bible Myth: The African Origins of the Jewish People*. Secaucus, NJ: Citadel Press, 1996.
——. *101 Myths of the Bible: How Ancient Scribes Invented Biblical History*. Naperville, IL: Sourcebooks, 2000.
Grimal, Pierre. *The Penguin Dictionary of Classical Mythology*. 1951. Harmondsworth, UK: Penguin, 1990 ed.
Grotjahn, Martin. *The Voice of the Symbol*. Los Angeles, CA: Mara Books, 1971.
Gruss, Edmond C. *What Every Mormon Should Know*. 1975. Denver, CO: Accent, 1976 ed.
Guignebert, Charles. *The Christ*. 1943. New York, NY: Citadel, 1968 ed.
Guthrie, William K. C. *The Greeks and Their Gods*. Boston, MA: Beacon Press, 1955.
Hadas, Moses (ed.). *A History of Rome*. Garden City, NY: Doubleday Anchor, 1956.
Haining, Peter. *Witchcraft and Black Magic*. New York, NY: Grosset and Dunlap, 1972.
Hall, Eleanor L. *The Moon and the Virgin: Reflections on the Archetypal Feminine*. New York, NY: Harper and Row, 1980.
Hall, John Richard Clark. *A Concise Anglo-Saxon Dictionary*. 1894. Toronto, Canada: University of Toronto Press, 1996 ed.
Hall, Manly P. *The Secret Teachings of All Ages*. 1925. Los Angeles, CA: The Philosophical Research Society, 1989 ed.
Halliday, William Reginald. *Greek and Roman Folklore*. New York, NY: Cooper Square, 1963.
Hamilton, Edith. *The Greek Way*. 1930. New York, NY: Mentor, 1959 ed.
——. *The Roman Way*. 1932. New York, NY: Mentor, 1961 ed.
——. *Mythology: Timeless Tales of Gods and Heroes*. 1940. New York, NY: Mentor, 1963 ed.
Hardon, John A. *Pocket Catholic Dictionary*. 1980. New York, NY: Image, 1985 ed.
Harrison, Michael. *The Roots of Witchcraft*. Secaucus, NJ: Citadel Press, 1974.
Hart, Donna, and Robert W. Sussman. *Man the Hunted: Primates, Predators, and Human Evolution*. Boulder, CO: Westview Press, 2008.
Haskins, Susan. *Mary Magdalene: Myth and Metaphor*. New York, NY: Harcourt Brace, 1993.
Heidel, Alexander. *The Gilgamesh Epic and Old Testament Parallels*. Chicago, IL: University of Chicago Press, 1949.
Heindel, Max. *Nature Spirits and Nature Forces*. Oceanside, CA: Rosicrucian Fellowship, 1937.
Herm, Gerhard. *The Celts: The People Who Came Out of the Darkness*. New York, NY: St. Martin's Press, 1976.
Hinnells, John R. (ed.). *Persian Mythology*. London, UK: Hamlyn, 1973.
——. *The Penguin Dictionary of Religions: From Abraham to Zoroaster*. 1984. Harmondsworth, UK: Penguin, 1986 ed.
Hite, Shere. *The Hite Report: A National Study of Female Sexuality*. 1976. New York, NY: Seven Stories Press, 1981 ed.
——. *The Hite Report on Male Sexuality*. New York, NY: Ballantine, 1987.
Hobson, Barbara Meil. *Uneasy Virtue: The Politics of Prostitution and the American Reform Tradition*. 1987. Chicago, IL: University of Chicago Press, 1990 ed.
Hodson, Geoffrey. *The Hidden Wisdom in the Holy Bible*. Vol. 1. 1967. Wheaton, IL: Quest, 1978 ed.

———. *The Hidden Wisdom in the Holy Bible.* Vol. 2. 1967. Wheaton, IL: Quest, 1978 ed.
Hoeller, Stephan A. *Jung and the Lost Gospels: Insights into the Dead Sea Scrolls and the Nag Hammadi Library.* 1989. Wheaton, IL: Quest, 1990 ed.
Hoffman, Barry (ed.). *Gauntlet: Exploring the Limits of Free Expression* (see "In Defense of Prostitution," No. 7). Colorado Springs, CO: Gauntlet Press, 1994.
Hollander, Xaviera. *The Happy Hooker: My Own Story.* New York, NY: Dell, 1973.
Holroyd, Stuart. *The Arkana Dictionary of New Perspectives.* Harmondsworth, UK: Arkana, 1989.
Hooke, S. K. *Middle Eastern Mythology: From the Assyrians to the Hebrews.* 1963. Harmondsworth, UK: Penguin, 1991 ed.
Hopfe, Lewis M. *Religions of the World.* 1976. New York, NY: Macmillan, 1987 ed.
Hoyland, Robert G. *Arabia and the Arabs: From the Bronze Age to the Coming of Islam.* London, UK: Routledge, 2001.
Hrdy, Sarah Blaffer. *Mother Nature: Maternal Instincts and How They Shape the Human Species.* New York, NY: Ballantine, 1999.
Hutchinson, Richard Wyatt. *Prehistoric Crete.* 1962. Harmondsworth, UK: Penguin, 1968 ed.
Hutton, Ronald. *The Pagan Religions of the Ancient British Isles: Their Nature and Legacy.* 1991. Oxford, UK: Blackwell, 2000 ed.
Huxley, Francis. *The Way of the Sacred.* New York, NY: Doubleday, 1974.
Ide, Arthur Frederick. *Yahweh's Wife: Sex in the Evolution of Monotheism.* Las Colinas, TX: Monument Press, 1991.
Jabbar, Mailk H. *The Astrological Foundation of the Christ Myth.* 4 vols. Dayton, OH: Rare Books Distributor, 1995-2003.
Jackson, John G. *Christianity Before Christ.* Austin, TX: American Atheist Press, 1985.
James, Peter, and Nick Thorpe. *Ancient Inventions.* New York, NY: Ballantine, 1994.
Jeffreys, Sheila. *The Idea of Prostitution.* North Melbourne, Australia: Spinifex Press, 1997.
———. *The Industrial Vagina: The Political Economy of the Global Sex Trade.* New York, NY: Routledge, 2009.
Jenness, Valerie. *Making It Work: The Prostitute's Rights Movement in Perspective.* Piscataway, NJ: Aldine Transaction, 1993.
Johanson, Donald. *Lucy: The Beginnings of Humankind.* New York, NY: Touchstone, 1981.
Johns, June. *Black Magic Today.* London, UK: New English Library, 1971.
Johnson, Robert A. *She: Understanding Feminine Psychology.* 1976. New York, NY: Perennial, 1977 ed.
Johnson, Walter, and William Wright. *Neolithic Man in North-East Surrey.* London, UK: Elliot Stock, 1903.
Jonas, Hans. *The Gnostic Religion: The Message of the Alien God and the Beginnings of Christianity.* 1958. Boston, MA: Beacon Press, 2001 ed.
Jones, Gwyn. *A History of the Vikings.* 1968. Oxford, UK: Oxford University Press, 1984 ed.
Jones, Prudence, and Nigel Pennick. *A History of Pagan Europe.* London, UK: Routledge, 1995.
Josephus: Complete Works. Circa 1st to 2nd Centuries C.E. Grand Rapids, MI: Kregel Publications, 1960, 1980 ed.

Julian of Norwich. *Revelations of Divine Love.* 1373. Harmondsworth, UK: Penguin, 1966 ed.
Jung, Carl Gustav. *Man and His Symbols.* 1964. New York, NY: Dell, 1968 ed.
Jurmain, Robert, Lynn Kilgore, and Wenda Trevathan. *Essentials of Physical Anthropology.* Belmont, CA: Wadsworth, 2009.
Keller, Werner. *The Bible As History: A Confirmation of the Book of Books.* 1956. New York, NY: Bantam, 1980 ed.
Kelly, Sean, and Rosemary Rogers. *Saints Preserve Us!: Everything You Need to Know About Every Saint You'll Ever Need.* New York, NY: Randon House, 1993.
Kelsey, Morton T., and Barbara Kelsey. *Sacrament of Sexuality: The Spirituality and Psychology of Sex.* Warwick, NY: Amity House, 1986.
Kempadoo, Kamala, and Jo Doezema (eds.). *Global Sex Workers: Rights, Resistance, and Redefinition.* New York, NY: Routledge, 1998.
Kempadoo, Kamala, Jyoti Sanqhera, and Bandana Pattanaik (eds.). *Trafficking and Prostitution Reconsidered: New Perspectives on Migration, Sex Work, and Human Rights.* Boulder, CO: Paradigm, 2005.
Kinsey, Alfred C., Wardell B. Pomeroy, and Clyde E. Martin. *Sexual Behavior in the Human Male.* 1948. Bloomington, IN: Indiana University Press, 1975 ed.
Kinsley, David. *The Goddesses' Mirror: Visions of the Divine From East and West.* Albany, NY: State University of New York Press, 1989.
Kirk, G. S. *The Nature of the Greek Myths.* 1974. Harmondsworth, UK: Penguin, 1978 ed.
Klein, Peter (ed.). *The Catholic Source Book.* Dubuque, IA: Brown-Roa, 2000.
Knight, Richard Payne. *A Discourse on the Worship of Priapus, and Its Connection With the Mystic Theology of the Ancients.* London, UK: privately printed, 1865 ed.
——. *The Symbolic Language of Ancient Art and Mythology.* New York, NY: J. W. Bouton, 1892.
Knight, Sirona. *Exploring Celtic Druidism: Ancient Magick and Rituals for Personal Empowerment.* Franklin Lakes, NJ: Career Press, 2001.
Kolodny, Robert, Virginia E. Johnson, and William H. Masters. *Masters and Johnson on Sex and Human Loving.* Boston, MA: Little, Brown, and Co., 1988.
Koran, The (George Sale, trans.). 1734. London, UK: Frederick Warne, n.d.
Kottak, Conrad. *Anthropology: The Exploration of Human Diversity.* Chicago, IL: McGraw-Hill, 2008.
Kramarae, Cheris, and Paula A. Treichler. *A Feminist Dictionary.* Champaign, IL: University of Illinois Press, 1996.
Kramer, Heinrich, and Jakob Sprenger. *Malleus Maleficarum.* 1486. New York, NY: Dover, 1971.
Kramer, Samuel Noah. *History Begins at Sumer: Thirty-Nine Firsts in Recorded History.* 1956. Philadelphia, PA: University of Pennsylvania Press, 1981 ed.
Kuhn, Alvin Boyd. *A Rebirth For Christianity.* 1970. Wheaton, IL: Quest, 2005.
Lacy, Norris J. (ed.). *The Arthurian Encyclopedia.* New York, NY: Garland Publishing, 1986.
Laistner, Max Ludwig Wolfram. *Christianity and Pagan Culture in the Later Roman Empire.* Ithaca, NY: Cornell University Press, 1951.
Lamsa, George M. *The Holy Bible: From Ancient Eastern Manuscripts.* 1933. Philadelphia, PA: A. J. Holman, 1968 ed.

Langum, David J. *Crossing Over the Line: Legislating Morality and the Mann Act.* 1994. Chicago, IL: University of Chicago Press, 2006 ed.
Larousse Encyclopedia of Mythology, New. 1959. London, UK: Hamlyn, 1976 ed.
Lass, Abraham H., David Kiremidjian, and Ruth M. Goldstein. *The Dictionary of Classical, Biblical, and Literary Allusions.* New York, NY: Fawcett Gold Medal, 1987.
LaVey, Anton Szandor. *The Satanic Bible.* New York, NY: Avon, 1969.
Layton, Bentley. *The Gnostic Scriptures: Ancient Wisdom for the New Age.* 1987. New York, NY: Anchor, 1995 ed.
Leakey, Richard E., and Roger Lewin. *Origins Reconsidered: In Search of What Makes Us Human.* New York, NY: Doubleday, 1992.
Leeming, David Adams. *The World of Myth.* 1990. Oxford, UK: Oxford University Press, 1992 ed.
——. *Jealous Gods and Chosen People: The Mythology of the Middle East.* New York, NY: Oxford University Press, 2004.
Legge, Francis. *Forerunners and Rivals of Christianity.* 2 vols. New York, NY: University Books, 1964.
Leigh, Carol. *Unrepentant Whore: Collected Works of Scarlot Harlot.* San Francisco, CA: Last Gasp, 2004.
LeLoup, Jean-Yves. *The Gospel of Mary Magdalene.* Rochester, VT: Inner Traditions, 2002.
——. *The Gospel of Philip: Jesus, Mary Magdalene, and the Gnosis of Sacred Union.* Rochester, VT: Inner Traditions, 2004.
——. *The Gospel of Thomas: The Gnostic Wisdom of Jesus.* Rochester, VT: Inner Traditions, 2005.
Lerner, Gerda. *The Creation of Patriarchy.* 1986. Oxford, UK: Oxford University Press, 1987 ed.
Levi. *The Aquarian Gospel of Jesus the Christ: The Philosophic and Practical Basis of the Religion of the Aquarian Age of the World and of the Church Universal.* Marina Del Ray, CA: DeVorss and Co., 1982.
Lewis, Harvey Spencer. *Mansions of the Soul: The Cosmic Conception.* 1930. San Jose, CA: Ancient Mystical Order Rosae Crucis (AMORC), 1969 ed.
Ley, David J. *Insatiable Wives: Women Who Stray and the Men Who Love Them.* Lanham, MD: Rowman and Littlefield, 2009.
Lilly, William. *Christian Astrology.* 3 vols. 1647. New York, NY: Cosimo, 2005 ed.
Lindsay, Jack. *The Origins of Astrology.* New York, NY: Barnes and Noble, 1971.
Littleton, C. Scott (ed). *Mythology: The Illustrated Anthology of World Myth and Storytelling.* London, UK: Duncan Baird Publishers, 2002.
Lockyer, Herbert. *All the Women of the Bible.* Grand Rapids, MI: Zondervan, n.d.
Loetscher, Lefferts A. (ed.-in-chief). *Twentieth Century Encyclopedia of Religious Knowledge.* 2 vols. Grand Rapids, MI: Baker Book House, 1955.
Lost Books of the Bible and the Forgotten Books of Eden, The. World Bible Publishers, 1926.
Ludlow, Daniel H. (ed.). *Encyclopedia of Mormonism: The History, Scripture, Doctrine, and Procedure of the Church of Jesus Christ of Latter-Day Saints.* New York, NY: Macmillan, 1992.
Lurker, Manfred. *The Gods and Symbols of Ancient Egypt.* 1974. New York, NY: Thames and Hudson, 1984 ed.

———. *Dictionary of Gods and Goddesses, Devils and Demons*. 1984. London, UK: Routledge, 1988 ed.
MacCana, Proinsias. *Celtic Mythology*. London, UK: Hamlyn, 1970.
MacLysaght, Edward. *The Surnames of Ireland*. 1985. Dublin, Ireland: Irish Academic Press, 1999 ed.
Malachi, Tau. *Gnosis of the Cosmic Christ: A Gnostic Christian Kabbalah*. St. Paul, MN: Llewellyn, 2005.
———. *Living Gnosis: A Practical Guide to Gnostic Christianity*. St. Paul, MN: Llewellyn, 2005.
———. *St. Mary Magdalene: The Gnostic Tradition of the Holy Bride*. St. Paul, MN: Llewellyn, 2006.
Mann, Nicholas R. *The Isle of Avalon: Sacred Mysteries of Arthur and Glastonbury*. London, UK: Green Magic, 2001.
Marcus, Rebecca B. *Prehistoric Cave Paintings*. New York, NY: Franklin Watts, 1968.
Markale, Jean. *Cathedral of the Black Madonna: The Druids and the Mysteries of Chartres*. Rochester, VT: Inner Traditions, 2004.
Marrs, Jim. *Alien Agenda: Investigating the Extraterrestrial Presence Among Us*. New York, NY: Harper Collins, 1997.
Maspero, Gaston. *Popular Stories of Ancient Egypt*. New York, NY: University Books, 1967.
Massey, Gerald. *The Historical Jesus, and the Mythical Christ: Natural Genesis and Typology of Equinoctial Christolatry*. 1883. New York, NY: Cosimo, 2006 ed.
———. *Ancient Egypt: The Light of the World*. 12 vols. London, UK: T. Fisher Unwin, 1907.
Masters, William H. *Human Sexual Response*. Philadelphia, PA: Lippincott Williams and Wilkins, 1966.
Matrix, Cherie (ed.). *Tales From the Clit: A Female Experience of Pornography*. Oakland, CA: AK Press, 2001.
Matthews, Caitlín, and John Matthews. *The Encyclopedia of Celtic Wisdom: A Celtic Shaman's Sourcebook*. Rockport, MA: Element, 1994.
Matthews, John. *The Winter Solstice: The Sacred Traditions of Christmas*. Wheaton, IL: Quest, 2003.
Maverick, Michelle. *Diary of a Legal Prostitute*. Boca Raton, FL: Universal Publishers, 2004.
McArthur, Tom (ed.). *The Oxford Companion to the English Language*. Oxford, UK: Oxford University Press, 1992.
McConkie, Bruce R. *Mormon Doctrine*. 1966. Salt Lake City, UT: Bookcraft, 1992 ed.
McKenzie, John L. *Dictionary of the Bible*. New York, NY: Collier, 1965.
McKinsey, C. Dennis. *The Encyclopedia of Biblical Errancy*. Amherst, NY: Prometheus, 1995.
McLean, Adam (ed.). *A Treatise on Angel Magic: Magnum Opus Hermetic Sourceworks*. 1989. York Beach, ME: Weiser, 2006 ed.
Mead, George Robert Stow. *Thrice-Greatest Hermes: Studies in Hellenistic Theosophy and Gnosis*. London, UK: Theosophical Publishing Society, 1906.
———. *The Mysteries of Mithra*. London, UK: Theosophical Publishing Society, 1907.
Mead, Frank Spencer, and Samuel S. Hill. *Handbook of Denominations in the United States*. 1951. Nashville, TN: Abingdon Press, 1989 ed.
Mead, Margaret. *Coming of Age in Samoa: A Psychological Study of Primitive Youth for Western Civilization*. New York, NY: William Morrow and Co., 1928.

———. *Growing Up in New Guinea: A Comparative Study of Primitive Education*. New York, NY: William Morrow and Co., 1930.
———. *Sex and Temperament in Three Primitive Societies*. New York, NY: William Morrow and Co., 1935.
———. *Male and Female: A Study of the Sexes in a Changing World*. New York, NY: William Morrow and Co., 1949.
———. *Letters From the Field, 1925-1975*. New York, NY: Harper and Row, 1977.
Meaden, George Terence. *The Goddess of the Stones: The Language of the Megaliths*. London, UK: Souvenir Press, 1990.
Meredith, Joel. *Meredith's Book of Bible Lists*. Minneapolis, MN: Bethany House, 1980.
Meretrix, Magdalene. *Turning Pro: A Guide to Sex Work for the Ambitious and the Intrigued*. Oakland, CA: Greenery Press, 2001.
Metford, J. C. J. *Dictionary of Christian Lore and Legend*. London, UK: Thames and Hudson, 1983.
Metzger, Bruce M., and Michael D. Coogan (eds.). *The Oxford Companion to the Bible*. New York, NY: Oxford University Press, 1993.
Meurois-Givaudan, Anne and Daniel. *The Way of the Essenes: Christ's Hidden Life Remembered*. Rochester, VT: Destiny, 1992.
Meyers, Carol (gen. ed.). *Women in Scripture: A Dictionary of Named and Unnamed Women in the Hebrew Bible, the Apocryphal/Deuterocanonical Books, and the New Testament*. 2000. Grand Rapids, MI: William B. Eerdmans, 2001 ed.
Miller, Malcolm. *Chartres Cathedral*. New York, NY: Riverside Book Co., 1997.
Miller, Robert J. (ed.). *The Complete Gospels* (Annotated Scholars Version). Sonoma, CA: Polebridge Press, 1994.
Millet, Kate. *Sexual Politics*. 1969. Chicago, IL: University of Illinois Press, 2000 ed.
Mills, A. D. *Oxford Dictionary of English Place-names*. 1991. Oxford, UK: Oxford University Press, 1998 ed.
Mish, Frederick (ed.). *Webster's Ninth New Collegiate Dictionary*. Springfield, MA: Merriam-Webster, 1984 ed.
Mollenkott, Virginia Ramey. *The Divine Feminine: The Biblical Imagery of God as Female*. New York, NY: Crossroad Publishing, 1993.
Monaghan, Patricia. *The Book of Goddesses and Heroines*. 1990. St. Paul, MN: Llewellyn, 1991 ed.
Monroe, Douglas. *The 21 Lessons of Merlyn: A Study in Druid Magic and Lore*. St. Paul, MN: Llewellyn, 1992.
Montagu, Ashley. *The Natural Superiority of Women*. 1952. New York, NY: Collier, 1992 ed.
Morehead, Albert H. (ed.). *The Illustrated World Encyclopedia*. 1954. Woodbury, NY: Bobley Publishing, 1977 ed.
Morgan, Elaine. *The Descent of Woman: The Classic Study of Evolution*. 1972. New York, NY: Bantam, 1973 ed.
Morris, Desmond. *The Naked Ape: A Zoologist's Study of the Human Animal*. New York, NY: Dell, 1967.
———. *The Human Zoo: A Zoologist's Classic Study of the Urban Animal*. New York, NY: Random House, 1969.
———. *Intimate Behavior: A Zoologist's Classic Study of Human Intimacy*. New York, NY: Random House, 1971.

———. *The Naked Woman: A Study of the Female Body*. New York, NY: Thomas Dunne, 2004.
———. *The Naked Man: A Study of the Male Body*. New York, NY: Thomas Dunne, 2009.
Nagle, Jill (ed.). *Whores and Other Feminists*. New York, NY: Routledge, 1997.
Nelson, Thomas (pub.). *Nelson's New Compact Illustrated Bible Dictionary*. 1964. Nashville, TN: Thomas Nelson, 1978 ed.
Neumann, Erich. *The Great Mother: An Analysis of the Archetype*. New York, NY: Pantheon, 1955.
Newall, Venetia. *The Encyclopedia of Witchcraft and Magic*. A and W Visual Library, 1974.
Norton-Taylor, Duncan. *The Emergence of Man: The Celts*. New York, NY: Time-Life, 1974.
Nystrom, Pia. *The Life of Primates*. Upper Saddle River, NJ: Prentice Hall, 2008.
Oakley, Annie (ed.). *Working Sex: Sex Workers Write About a Changing Industry*. Emeryville, CA: Seal Press, 2007.
O'Brien, Arthur. *Europe Before Modern Times: An Ancient and Medieval History*. 1940. Chicago, IL: Loyola University Press, 1943 ed.
Odent, Michael. *Water and Sexuality*. Harmondsworth, UK: Arkana, 1990.
O'Flaherty, Wendy Doniger. *Hindu Myths*. Harmondsworth, UK: Penguin, 1975.
Olson, Carl (ed.). *The Book of the Goddess, Past and Present: An Introduction to Her Religion*. New York, NY: Crossroad, 1983.
Orme, A. R. *Ireland*. Chicago, IL: Aldine, 1970.
Osborne, John. *Britain*. New York, NY: Time-Life, 1963.
Oxford English Dictionary, The (compact edition, 2 vols.). 1928. Oxford, UK: Oxford University Press, 1979 ed.
Pagels, Elaine. *The Gnostic Gospels*. 1979. New York, NY: Vintage, 1981 ed.
———. *Adam, Eve, and the Serpent*. 1988. New York, NY: Vintage, 1989 ed.
———. *The Origin of Satan*. New York, NY: Random House, 1995.
Patai, Raphael. *The Hebrew Goddess*. 1967. Detroit, MI: Wayne State University Press, 1990 ed.
Paulsen, Kathryn. *The Complete Book of Magic and Witchcraft*. 1970. New York, NY: Signet, 1980 ed.
Pearson, Carol S. *Awakening the Heroes Within: Twelve Archetypes to Help Us Find Ourselves and Transform Our World*. New York, NY: HarperCollins, 1991.
Pennick, Nigel. *The Pagan Book of Days: A Guide to the Festivals, Traditions, and Sacred Days of the Year*. Rochester, VT: Destiny, 1992.
Pepper, Elizabeth, and John Wilcock. *Magical and Mystical Sites: Europe and the British Isles*. Grand Rapids, MI: Phanes Press, 1992.
Perkins, Roberta, and Garrett Prestage (eds.). *Sex Work and Sex Workers in Australia*. Kensington, NSW: University of New South Wales, 1994.
Perowne, Stewart. *Roman Mythology*. 1969. Twickenham, UK: Newnes Books, 1986 ed.
Pheterson, Gail (ed.). *A Vindication of the Rights of Whores: The International Movement for Prostitutes' Rights*. Seattle, WA: Seal Press, 1989.
———. *The Prostitution Prism*. Amsterdam, The Netherlands: Amsterdam University Press, 1996.

Pinch, Geraldine. *Egyptian Mythology: A Guide to the Gods, Goddesses, and Traditions of Ancient Egypt*. Oxford, UK: Oxford University Press, 2004.

Pisani, Elizabeth. *The Wisdom of Whores: Bureaucrats, Brothels and the Business of AIDS*. New York, NY: W. W. Norton, 2008.

Prahbupada, A. C. Bhaktivedanta Swami. *Beyond Birth and Death*. Los Angeles, CA: The Bhaktivedanta Book Trust, 1979.

Prophet, Elizabeth Clare. *Mary Magdalene and the Divine Feminine: Jesus' Lost Teachings on Woman - How Orthodoxy Suppressed Jesus' Revolution for Woman and Invented Original Sin*. Gardiner, MT: Summit University Press, 2005.

Qualls-Corbett, Nancy. *The Sacred Prostitute: Eternal Aspect of the Feminine*. Toronto, Canada: Inner City Books, 1988.

Quan, Tracy. *Diary of a Manhattan Call Girl*. New York, NY: Three Rivers Press, 2001.

Queen, Carol. *Real Live Nude Girl: Chronicles of Sex-Positive Culture*. San Francisco, CA: Cleis Press, 2002.

Raftery, Barry. *Pagan Celtic Ireland: The Enigma of the Irish Iron Age*. London, UK: Thames and Hudson, 1994.

Ramm, Bernard L. *Hermeneutics*. 1967. Grand Rapids, MI: Baker Book House, 1988 ed.

Reaney, P. H. *Oxford Dictionary of English Surnames*. 1958. Oxford, UK: Oxford University Press, 1997 ed.

Redmond, Ian. *The Primate Family Tree: The Amazing Diversity of Our Closest Relatives*. Buffalo, NY: Firefly, 2008.

Reed, Ellen Cannon. *Circle of Isis: Ancient Egyptian Magic for Modern Witches*. Franklin Lakes, NJ: Career Press, 2002.

Regula, deTraci. *The Mysteries of Isis: Her Worship and Magick*. 1995. St. Paul, MN: Llewellyn, 2001 ed.

Reilly, Patricia Lynn. *A God Who Looks Like Me: Discovering a Woman-Affirming Spirituality*. New York, NY: Ballantine, 1995.

Reinisch, June M., and Ruth Beasley. *The Kinsey Institute New Report on Sex: What You Must Know to Be Sexually Literate*. New York, NY: St. Martin's Press, 1990.

Ringdal, Nils Johan. *Love For Sale: A World History of Prostitution*. 1997. New York, NY: Grove Press, 2004 ed.

Roberts, J. D. *The Business Side of Escorting: The Ins and Outs of Running a Business in the Cyber Age for the Escort and the Sensual Masseuse Serious About Her Profession*. Lincoln, NE: iUniverse, 2004.

Roberts, Nickie. *Whores in History: Prostitution in Western Society*. San Francisco, CA: HarperCollins, 1992.

Roberts, R. Philip. *Mormonism Unmasked: Confronting the Contradictions Between Mormon Beliefs and True Christianity*. Nashville, TN: Broadman and Holman, 1998.

Robertson, John M. *Christianity and Mythology*. London, UK: Watts and Co., 1900.

——. *A Short History of Christianity*. London, UK: Watts and Co., 1902.

——. *Pagan Christs: Studies in Comparative Hierology*. London, UK: Watts and Co., 1903.

——. *Pagan Christs*. 1966. New York, NY: Dorset Press, 1987 ed.

Robertson, Judy. *Out of Mormonism: A Woman's True Story*. 1997. Bloomington, MN: Bethany House, 2001 ed.

Robinson, James M (ed.). *The Nag Hammadi Library in English*. 1978. San Francisco, CA: HarperCollins, 1990 ed.

Rocco, Sha. *Sex Mythology*. 1898. Austin, TX: American Atheist Press, 1982 ed.

Rosen, Ruth. *The Lost Sisterhood: Prostitution in America, 1900-1918.* Baltimore, MD: John Hopkins University Press, 1982.

Rufus, Anneli S., and Kristan Lawson. *Goddess Sites: Europe.* New York, NY: HarperCollins, 1991.

Runciman, Steven. *A History of the Crusades: Vol. 1, The First Crusade and the Foundation of the Kingdom of Jerusalem.* 1951. New York, NY: Harper Torchbooks, 1964 ed.

Runes, Dagobert D. (ed.). *Dictionary of Judaism.* 1959. New York, NY: Citadel Press, 1991 ed.

Russell, Bertrand. *Why I Am Not a Christian: and Other Essays on Religion and Related Subjects.* New York, NY: Touchstone, 1957.

Rutherford, Ward. *Celtic Mythology: The Nature and Influence of Celtic Myth - From Druidism to Arthurian Legend.* New York, NY: Sterling, 1990.

Ryan, Christopher, and Cacilda Jethá. *Sex at Dawn: The Prehistoric Origins of Modern Sexuality.* New York, NY: Harper, 2010.

Salmonson, Jessica Amanda. *The Encyclopedia of Amazons: Women Warriors from Antiquity to the Modern Era.* New York, NY: Paragon House, 1991.

Sapolsky, Robert M. *A Primate's Memoir: A Neuroscientist's Unconventional Life Among the Baboons.* New York, NY: Touchstone, 2001.

Schaller, George B. *The Year of the Gorilla.* 1964. Chicago, IL: University of Chicago Press, 1988 ed.

Schwartz, Howard. *Gabriel's Palace: Jewish Mystical Tales.* New York, NY: Oxford University Press, 1993.

——. *Tree of Souls: The Mythology of Judaism.* Oxford, UK: Oxford University Press, 2004.

Scott, Latayne C. *The Mormon Mirage: A Former Member Looks at the Mormon Church Today.* Grand Rapids, MI: Zondervan, 2009.

Seabrook, Lochlainn. *The Goddess Dictionary of Words and Phrases: Introducing a New Core Vocabulary for the Women's Spirituality Movement.* 1997. Nashville, TN: Sea Raven Press, 2010 ed.

——. *The Book of Kelle: An Introduction to Goddess-Worship and the Great Celtic Mother-Goddess Kelle, Original Blessed Lady of Ireland.* 1999. Franklin, TN: Sea Raven Press, 2010 ed.

——. *Britannia Rules: Goddess-Worship in Ancient Anglo-Celtic Society - An Academic Look at the United Kingdom's Matricentric Spiritual Past.* 1999. Franklin, TN: Sea Raven Press, 2010 ed.

——. *Princess Diana: Modern Day Moon-Goddess - A Psychoanalytical and Mythological Look at Diana Spencer's Life, Marriage, and Death* (with Dr. Jane Goldberg). Spring Hill, TN: Sea Raven Press, 2008.

——. *Abraham Lincoln: The Southern View - Demythologizing America's Sixteenth President.* Franklin, TN: Sea Raven Press, 2009.

——. *Christmas Before Christianity: How the Birthday of the "Sun" Became the Birthday of the "Son."* Franklin, TN: Sea Raven Press, 2010.

——. *Jesus and the Law of Attraction: The Bible-Based Guide to Creating Perfect Health, Wealth, and Happiness Following Christ's Simple Formula.* Spring Hill, TN: Sea Raven Press, 2013.

——. *The Bible and the Law of Attraction: 99 Teachings of Jesus, the Apostles, and the Prophets.* Spring Hill, TN: Sea Raven Press, 2013.

———. *Christ Is All and In All: Rediscovering Your Divine Nature and the Kingdom Within*. Spring Hill, TN: Sea Raven Press, 2014.
———. *Jesus and the Gospel of Q: Christ's Pre-Christian Teachings As Recorded in the New Testament*. Spring Hill, TN: Sea Raven Press, 2014.
———. *Autobiography of a Non-Yogi: A Scientist's Journey From Hinduism to Christianity* (Dr. Amitava Dasgupta and Lochlainn Seabrook). Spring Hill, TN: Sea Raven Press, 2015.
———. *Seabrook's Bible Dictionary of Traditional and Mystical Christian Doctrines*. Spring Hill, TN: Sea Raven Press, 2016.
———. *Women in Gray: A Tribute to the Ladies Who Supported the Southern Confederacy*. Spring Hill, TN: Sea Raven Press, 2016.
———. *The Concise Book of Owls: A Guide to Nature's Most Mysterious Birds*. Spring Hill, TN: Sea Raven Press, 2019.
———. *The Concise Book of Tigers: A Guide to Nature's Most Remarkable Cats*. Spring Hill, TN: Sea Raven Press, 2020.
Seagraves, Anne. *Soiled Doves: Prostitution in the Early West*. Hayden, ID: Wesanne Publications, 1994.
Seznec, Jean. *The Survival of the Pagan Gods*. Princeton, NJ: Princeton University Press, 1953.
Shah, Amina. *Arabian Fairy Tales*. London, UK: Octagon Press, 1989.
———. *Tales From the Bazaars of Arabia: Folk Stories From the Middle East*. London, UK: Octagon Press, 2002.
Shaner, Lora. *Madam: Inside a Nevada Brothel*. Las Vegas, NV: Huntington Press, 2003.
Shaw, Ian (ed.). *The Oxford History of Ancient Egypt*. 2000. Oxford, UK: Oxford University Press, 2002 ed.
Sherfey, Mary Jane. *The Nature and Evolution of Female Sexuality*. 1972. New York, NY: Vintage, 1973 ed.
Shrage, Laurie. *Moral Dilemmas of Feminism: Prostitution, Adultery, and Abortion*. New York, NY: Routledge, 1994.
Simons, Gerald. *Barbarian Europe* (from the *Great Ages of Man* series). New York, NY: Time-Life, 1968.
Sjöö, Monica, and Barbara Mor. *The Great Cosmic Mother: Rediscovering the Religion of the Earth*. New York, NY: Harper and Row, 1987.
Skelton, Robin, and Margaret Blackwood. *Earth, Air, Fire, Water: Pre-Christian and Pagan Elements in British Songs, Rhymes and Ballads*. Harmondsworth, UK: Arkana, 1990.
Smith, Lacey Baldwin. *This Realm of England: 1399 to 1688*. 1966. Lexington, MA: D. C. Heath and Co., 1983 ed.
Smith, William. *Smith's Bible Dictionary*. Circa 1880s. Nashville, TN: Thomas Nelson, 1986 ed.
Sobol, Donald J. *The Amazons of Greek Mythology*. Cranbury, NJ: A. S. Barnes and Co., 1972.
Spence, Lewis. *Ancient Egyptian Myths and Legends*. 1915. New York, NY: Dover, 1990 ed.
———. *An Encyclopedia of Occultism*. 1920. New York, NY: Citadel Press, 1993 ed.
———. *The History and Origins of Druidism*. 1949. New York, NY: Samuel Weiser, 1971 ed.
Spencer, James. *Beyond Mormonism: An Elder's Story*. Ada, MI: Chosen Books, 1984.

Sprinkle, Annie. *Annie Sprinkle: Post-Porn Modernist.* San Francisco, CA: Cleis Press, 1998.
Stanford, Craig, John S. Allen, and Susan C. Anton. *Biological Anthropology: The Natural History of Humankind.* Englewood Cliffs, NJ: Prentice Hall, 2005.
Starbird, Margaret. *The Goddess in the Gospels: Reclaiming the Sacred Feminine.* Rochester, VT: Bear and Co., 1998.
——. *Magdalene's Lost Legacy: Symbolic Numbers and the Sacred Union in Christianity.* Rochester, VT: Bear and Co., 2003.
Stark, Rodney. *Discovering God: The Origins of the Great Religions and the Evolution of Belief.* New York, NY: HarperCollins, 2007.
Stein, Diane. *The Goddess Book of Days.* 1988. Freedom, CA: The Crossing Press, 1992 ed.
Stein, Rebecca, and Philip L. Stein. *Anthropology of Religion, Magic, and Witchcraft.* Upper Saddle River, NJ: Allyn and Bacon, 2007.
Stetkevych, Jaroslav. *Muhammad and the Golden Bough: Reconstructing Arabian Myth.* Bloomington, IN: Indiana University Press, 1996.
Stone, Merlin. *When God was a Woman.* San Diego, CA: Harvest, 1976.
——. *Ancient Mirrors of Womanhood: A Treasury of Goddess and Heroine Lore from Around the World.* 1979. Boston, MA: Beacon Press, 1990 ed.
Strachan, Gordon. *Chartres: Sacred Geometry, Sacred Space.* Edinburgh, Scotland: Floris Books, 2003.
Streep, Peg. *Sanctuaries of the Goddess: The Sacred Landscapes and Objects.* Boston, MA: Bullfinch Press, 1994.
Strieber, Whitley. *Communion: A True Story.* New York, NY: Avon, 1987.
——. *Transformation: The Breakthrough.* New York, NY: Avon, 1997.
——. *Confirmation: The Hard Evidence of Aliens Among Us.* New York, NY: St. Martin's Press, 1998.
Strier, Karen B. *Primate Behavioral Ecology.* Boston, MA: Allyn and Bacon, 2006 ed.
Strong, James. *Strong's Exhaustive Concordance of the Bible.* 1890. Nashville, TN: Abingdon Press, 1975 ed.
Stubbs, Kenneth Ray (ed.). *Women of the Light: The New Sacred Prostitute.* Traverse City, MI: Access Publishers Network, 1994.
Sturluson, Snorri. *The Prose Edda.* Berkeley, CA: University of California Press, 1954.
Swindoll, Cynthia (ed.). *Abraham: Friend of God.* 1986. Fullerton, CA: Insight for Living, 1988 ed.
Sykes, Egerton. *Who's Who in Non-Classical Mythology.* 1952. New York, NY: Oxford University Press, 1993 ed.
Szekely, Edmond Bordeaux. *The Essene Gospel of Peace.* 1937. Nelson, B.C., Canada: International Biogenic Society, 1981 ed.
Telushkin, Rabbi Joseph. *Jewish Literacy.* New York, NY: William Morrow and Co., 1991.
Tenney, Merrill C. (gen. ed.). *Handy Dictionary of the Bible.* Grand Rapids, MI: Lamplighter, 1965.
The Epic of Gilgamesh (N. K. Sandars, ed.). Circa 3000 BCE. Harmondsworth, UK: Penguin, 1960 (1972 ed.).
The Fossil Record and Evolution. Collected articles from *Scientific American.* San Francisco, CA: W. H. Freeman and Co., 1982 ed.

The Golden Treasury of Myths and Legends (adapted by Anne Terry White). New York, NY: Golden Press, 1959.
Thompson Chain-Reference Bible, The. King James Version. Indianapolis: B. B. Kirkbride Bible Co., 1964.
Thompson, James Westfall, and Edgar Nathaniel Johnson. *An Introduction to Medieval Europe: 300-1500*. New York, NY: W. W. Norton, 1937.
Thompson, Shawn. *The Intimate Ape: Orangutans and the Secret Life of a Vanishing Species*. New York, NY: Citadel, 2010.
Thorsten, Geraldine. *God Herself: The Feminine Roots of Astrology*. New York, NY: Avon, 1981.
Tompkins, Peter. *Secrets of the Great Pyramid*. 1971. New York, NY: Harper Colophon, 1978 ed.
Tong, Benson. *Unsubmissive Women: Chinese Prostitutes in Nineteenth-Century San Francisco*. Norman, OK: University of Oklahoma Press, 1994.
Towns, Elmer L. *The Names of Jesus*. Denver, CO: Accent, 1987.
Traupman, John C. *The New College Latin and English Dictionary*. 1966. New York, NY: Bantam, 1988 ed.
——. *The Bantam New College German and English Dictionary*. 1981. New York, NY: Bantam, 1986 ed.
Trevelyan, George Macaulay. *History of England: Vol. 1, From the Earliest Times to the Reformation*. 1926. Garden City, NY: Anchor, 1952 ed.
Tripp, Edward. *The Meridian Handbook of Classical Mythology*. 1970. Harmondsworth, UK: Meridian, 1974 ed.
Turcan, Robert. *The Cults of the Roman Empire*. 1992. Oxford, UK: Blackwell, 2000 ed.
Udry, J. Richard. *The Social Context of Marriage*. 1966. Philadelphia, PA: J. B. Lippincott, 1974 ed.
Van De Mieroop, Marc. *A History of the Ancient Near East, ca. 3000-323 BC*. 2004. Oxford, UK: Blackwell, 2007 ed.
Vermaseren, Maarten J. *Cybele and Attis*. London, UK: Thames and Hudson, 1977.
Vermes, Geza (ed.). *The Dead Sea Scrolls in English*. 1962. Harmondsworth, UK: Penguin, 1987 ed.
von Daniken, Erich. *Chariots of the Gods?: Unsolved Mysteries of the Past*. 1968. New York, NY: Bantam, 1973 ed.
——. *Gods from Outer Space: Return to the Stars, or Evidence for the Impossible*. 1968. New York, NY: Bantam, 1974 ed.
Walker, Barbara G. *The Woman's Encyclopedia of Myths and Secrets*. San Francisco, CA: Harper and Row, 1983.
——. *The Crone: Woman of Age, Wisdom, and Power*. San Francisco, CA: Harper and Row, 1985.
——. *The Woman's Dictionary of Symbols and Sacred Objects*. San Francisco, CA: Harper and Row, 1988.
Walkowitz, Judith R. *Prostitution and Victorian Society: Women, Class, and the State*. Cambridge, UK: Cambridge University Press, 1980.
Walum, Laurel Richardson. *The Dynamics of Sex and Gender: A Sociological Perspective*. Chicago, IL: Rand McNally College Publishing, 1977.
Watts, Alan. *Behold the Spirit: A Study in the Necessity of Mystical Religion*. 1947. New York, NY: Random House, 1971 ed.

Way, George, and Romilly Squire. *Scottish Clan and Family Encyclopedia.* Glasgow, Scotland: HarperCollins, 1994.
Weigall, Arthur. *The Life and Times of Akhnaton: Pharaoh of Egypt.* London, UK: W. Blackwood and Sons, 1910.
———. *Wanderings in Anglo-Saxon Britain.* New York, NY: George H. Doran, 1926.
———. *The Paganism in Our Christianity.* New York, NY: G. P. Putnam's Sons, 1928.
White, Jon Manchip. *Ancient Egypt: Its Culture and History.* 1952. New York, NY: Dover, 1970 ed.
———. *Everyday Life in Ancient Egypt.* 1963. New York, NY: Perigree, 1980 ed.
White, R. J. *The Horizon Concise History of England.* New York, NY: American Heritage, 1971.
Wilde, Lady. *Irish Cures, Mystic Charms, and Superstitions.* New York, NY: Sterling Publishing, 1991.
Wilson, Edward O. *Sociobiology.* Cambridge, MA: Belknap Press, 1975.
———. *On Human Nature.* Cambridge, MA: Harvard University Press, 1978.
Wind, Edgar. *Pagan Mysteries in the Renaissance.* New York, NY: W. W. Norton, 1968.
Winick, Charles. *Dictionary of Anthropology.* Totowa, NJ: Littlefield, Adams and Co., 1970.
Winks, Robin W., Crane Brinton, John B. Christopher, and Robert Lee Wolff. *A History of Civilization, Vol. 1: Prehistory to 1715.* 1955. Englewood Cliffs, NJ: Prentice Hall, 1988 ed.
Witt, Reginald Eldred. *Isis in the Ancient World.* 1971. Baltimore, MD: John Hopkins University Press, 1997.
Wood, Charles L. *The Mormon Conspiracy: A Review of Present-Day and Historical Conspiracies to Mormonize America and the World.* Chula Vista, CA: Black Forest Press, 2004.
Woods, Vanessa. *Bonobo Handshake: A Memoir of Love and Adventure in the Congo.* New York, NY: Gotham, 2010.
Woolger, Jennifer Barker, and Roger J. Woolger. *The Goddess Within: A Guide to the Eternal Myths that Shape Women's Lives.* 1987. New York, NY: Fawcett Columbine, 1989.
Worthy, Jack B. *The Mormon Cult: A Former Missionary Reveals the Secrets of Mormon Mind Control.* Tucson, AZ: See Sharp Press, 2008.
Wright, John W. (ed.). *The Universal Almanac, 1994.* Kansas City, MO: Andrews and McMeel, 1993.
Young, Dudley. *Origins of the Sacred: The Ecstasies of Love and War.* 1991. New York, NY: Harper Perennial, 1992 ed.
Young, G. Douglas (gen. ed.). *Young's Compact Bible Dictionary.* 1984. Wheaton, IL: Tyndale House, 1989 ed.
Zaehner, R. C. (ed.) *Encyclopedia of the World's Religions.* 1959. New York, NY: Barnes and Noble, 1997 ed.
Zimmerman, J. E. *Dictionary of Classical Mythology.* New York, NY: Bantam, 1964.
Zimmerman, Mark. *Guide to Civil War Nashville.* Nashville, TN: Battle of Nashville Preservation Society, 2004.
Zondervan (publisher). *Zondervan Compact Bible Dictionary.* 1967. Grand Rapids, MI: Zondervan, 1993 ed.

INDEX

abba 66
Abbess 66
Abbeys 66
abdomen, pregnant 50
abhor 95
abnormal 95
Abraham 64
Abraham Lincoln: The Southern View (Seabrook) 67, 120
abuse 54, 95, 97
Adad 56
Adam 48
Adam and Eve 48
addict 95
adepts 60
Aditi 73
adjunct laborers, men as 44
Adonai 72
Adonis 41, 73
adoration 93
adulation 93
adult film actors 78
adultery 95, 121
adultress 89
advisor 93
affairs, far worse than prostitution 84
Africa 48
Africa, named after the Whore-Goddess Aphrodite 42
African prostitute, Moses marries 48
Age of Pisces, the 60
aggression 46
Akhenaten 65
Albania, named after a goddess 42
all-embracing love 65
all-female colleges 52
all-female communities 46
all-female council 44
all-female groups 33
all-female island communities 45
all-important role, of sex workers 80
all-male groups 33
all-male Jewish priesthood 50
all-woman Greek island community 45
Almighty, the 64
Almodovar, Norma Jean 25
amazing 2, 3, 60, 93, 119
Amazonian teachings 45
Amazonian warrioresses 45
American States 38, 77
Americans 2
amniotic fluid 42, 62
amulets 62
Anath 70
Anatolia 70

Anatolian Goddess-worship 70
ancient Christians 37
ancient civilization 40
ancient Egypt 40
ancient Egyptian drawings 33
ancient female whores 42
ancient Graeco-Roman times 43
ancient Greece 40
ancient historical records 76
ancient Jews 47
ancient pre-Christian world 41
ancient times 40
Ancient Whore Wisdom 13
ancient whore, roles of 43
ancient whores 44
androcentric customs 76
angel 89, 93, 116
angelic 93, 103
angels 15
angels of mercy, sex workers as 80
Anglo-Saxon Spring-Goddess 41
animal 18, 95, 109, 117
Animalia 100
Anna 57
anoint 42, 57, 93
anointed 57, 93
anointing 58
Antheus 56
Anthony, Mark 167
Anthropoidea 100
anthropological studies 32
anthropologists 21, 35, 53
anthropology 53, 72
anti-Goddess Christian males 71
anti-Goddess pogroms 61
anti-prostitution edicts 61
anti-woman campaign 52
aphrodisiac 42
aphrodisiac, word derives from Aphrodite 42
Aphrodite 7, 23, 41, 42, 56, 65, 69-71, 74, 80, 89
Aphrodite, etymology of her name 42
Aphrodite's daughter 89
Aphrodite's Daughters 79
Aphrodite's Trade 1, 3, 5, 6, 11, 17, 21-23, 27, 29, 31, 36, 66, 77, 79-81, 85, 87, 91
Aphrodite's Trade (Seabrook) 21-23
Apollo 74
apotheosis 93
April 21 49
Apsaras 41
Arabia 113, 121, 122
Arabic Goddess-worship 70, 73
Aramaic words 66
archaeological digs 63
archaeological evidence 62
archaeological findings 45
archaic humans 37

archetypal figures 72
archetypal maternal figure 66
archetypal Pagan Savior-Sun-God 41
archetypal symbols 48
archetypes 10, 53, 118
Ardipithecus 101
Aries 42
Army surgeons 67
art 63
Artemis 41
artifacts 63
Aryans 63
asexual marriage 37
Asherah 48, 49, 62, 70
Asherah's place in Judaism 50
Ashtoreth 49
Asklepios 48
assimilation of Pagan ideas and practices, by Christianity 75
Astarte 41, 49, 70
astrological charts 43
astrology 43, 75, 107, 115, 123
Athaliah 50
atheism 95
atheist 95, 105, 107, 113, 119
atheists 80
atheists, demonizing sex workers 80
Aton 65
atonement 93
Atthar 70, 73
Attis 41, 56, 123
attorneys, sympathetic to sex work industry 80
Australopithecus 101
Autobiography of a Non-Yogi (Dasgupta and Seabrook) 121
aversion 95
Baal 56, 64
Babylon 10, 40, 51, 70
Babylonia 70
Babylonian Goddess-worship 70
Bacchus 56
bachelorhoods 33
bad luck 51, 58
bagnio 92
baker's dozen 58
Balder 56
Baldwin, Matilda 167
Bali 56
Balili 56
banshee 89
baptism 71
baptism for the dead, Mormon belief in 71
basic mating pattern, our 32
Basina, Queen 59, 60
Bath Qol 49
Bathseheba 8, 59
Bathsheba 59
bawd 89

bawdyhouse 92
beauty 27, 93
Beddru 56
bedmate 89
befoul 95
beldame 89
Belenus 56
Beloved Disciple, the 60
best girl 89
Bet Boshet 51
betrayer 89
Bible 3, 38, 49, 57, 61, 62, 64, 70, 71, 74, 89, 104-106, 108-118, 120-124, 168, 169
biblical references to God as a maternal 61
biblical writers 74
big-game hunters, men as 54
big-game hunting, and sexual dimorphism 33, 54
big-game hunting, early men programmed for 33
bigotry 79
bimbo 89
biological determinism 39
biological primate past, our 79
biologically hardwired 79
biology 37, 45, 56
biology is destiny 33
birds 3, 121
birth canal 33
bitch 89, 95
blaspheme 95
blemish 95
bless 93
blessing 93
blood 41
blood, royal, and Jesus 59
body worship 7
bonding ritual 75
Bonobo, the 36
bordello 92
born again 59, 75
Boudicca, Queen 167
bound 39, 97
brain 32
brain power 32
brass 48
breasts 50
breathing 21
bride 60, 116, 123
Briffault, Robert S. 63
Bright and Morning star 74
Bright One 74
Bringer of Light 74
Britain, named after a goddess 42
Britannia Rules (Seabrook) 42, 120
Britomartis 48
broad 89
brood 62
brothel 92, 103, 121

brothels, Catholic	66
brotherhoods	33
brotherhoods, all-male	33
Buckley, William F., Jr.	18, 22, 87
Buddha	56
buggery	95
bund	61
Bunjil	56
burden of child rearing	34
burning bush	64
buttocks	50
B-girl	89
Caduceus	48
Caesar	106
call girl	89, 103, 119
call house	92
camp follower	89
Cana of Galilee	59
Canaan	103
candles	75
caretakers of time	43
caroling	75
carry on	67, 91
carvings	63
Casanova	89
castration	45
Catarrhini	100
Catholic authorities	60, 70, 74
Catholic Church	56, 66, 67
Catholic churches	69
Catholic Cult of Mary	66
Catholic Fathers	66
Catholicism	74
Catholics	42, 69, 71
Catholics, and Goddess-worship	69, 70
cathouse	92
cave	40, 51, 58, 71, 116
cave-dweller	51
celebration	75, 93
celestial	72, 74, 93
celibacy	37
celibate marriage	37
Celtic Goddess-worship	70, 73
center	71, 84
Chaldea	57
Chaldean words	57
champion	93
chariot	74
Charis	41
Charites	41, 66
charmer	93
chastity	81
chatelaine	89
cheapen	95
cheater	89
chief roles	42

child rearing, and sexual dimorphism 33
child rearing, early women programmed for 33
children 2, 17, 21, 32, 33, 38, 54, 59, 73, 75, 76, 98, 110
children, with multiple partners 32
chimpanzee 36
chimpanzee females 36
chimpanzee males 36
chimpanzees 31, 100
chippy 89
Chordata 100
chris 57, 73
Chrishna 41, 56
chrism 42, 57, 73
Christ 80
Christ Consciousness 80
Christ Is All and In All (Seabrook) 121
Christ, etymology of 57, 73, 74
Christian art 33
Christian Church 33, 37
Christian churches, Goddess temples converted to 52
Christian denominations and sects 75
Christian denominations, and Goddess-worship 70
Christian iconography 33
Christian legend 57
Christian mosaic 74
Christian mythographers 65, 71, 73
Christian mythology 56, 59
Christian patriarchies 61
Christian Sun-God, Jesus as the 41
Christian Underworld 71
Christianity . 3, 11, 21, 41, 52, 54, 56, 57, 66, 73-75, 85, 103, 105, 109-111, 113-116, 119-122, 124,
                                                                                                169
Christianity and Pagan Easter 41
Christianity's holy days 75
christianization 57, 65, 66
christianization of the Winter Solstice 75
Christians 61, 72, 74
Christians, demonizing sex workers 80
christing (anointing) rituals 73
christing ritual 57
Christmas 75
Christmas Before Christianity (Seabrook) 56, 75, 120
Christmas Eve 75
Christmas, Pagan aspects of 75
Christos 73
Christs, list of pre-Christian 56
chrs 57, 73
church 33, 37, 52, 56, 57, 61, 65-67, 70, 75, 85, 103-105, 107-109, 115, 120
Church Fathers 52, 56, 57, 61, 66
church membership 65
Church of Jesus Christ of Latter-Day Saints 70, 71
Church of Jesus Christ of Latter-Day Saints 70, 115
Church, the 75
churches 52, 69, 70, 75
Circe 89
cities, named after goddesses 42

Civil War, American 67
civilizations 40
Clinton, Bill 87
clock-makers 77
Clodion, King 59
close-knit community 46
clothed with the Sun 73
coach 93
Coatlicue 48
coed schools, inferior to single-gender schools 33
colleges 45
Collegia 45
combat zone 92
commerce 80
Common Era 52
Community of Israel 49, 62
compassion 46
composite-deity 62
concubinage 91
concubine 89
confidence 93
conservation 107
consort 65
consort bond 32
consort bonding 45
Constitution, the US 19, 83, 85
constitutional rights 19
contamination 95
contemporary men 37
contemporary Western prostitution 80
contemporary women 37
contractual sex 35
convents 66
core vocabulary 3, 120
corpus callosum, in women and men 54
corruption 40, 72, 95
Cosmic Consciousness 80
cosmic enlightenment 47
council of deities 64
courtesan 89
Creation myth 41, 48, 62
crescent-Moon shaped amulets 62
Crete, named after a goddess 42
criminals, sex workers as 81
crippled men 45
Criti 41, 56
Crone 57, 58, 123
Crone-Goddess 58
crown 73
crown chakra 80
Crown, the 80
crucifixion 41, 58
cruel 95
cruelty 80, 95
Crusade 3, 120
crystal balls 60

Cuba, named after a goddess 42
cuckoldry 91
Cult of Jesus 66
Cult of the Vulva 51
cults 10, 48, 123
culture 46
cultures 40, 105
curative powers 60
curse 14, 95
Cybele 123
Cyrus 56
Cytherean 93
da Vinci, Leonardo 60
Daly, Mary 107
damnation 95
dance 45
dancers 78
dancing temple hors 78
Danebod, Thyra 167
dangers and hazards of men 45
Danu 103
Dark Moon 58
Dark Mother 71
darkness 79, 112
dating 32
daughter 13, 46, 50, 59, 61, 89
daughter of Aphrodite 89
daughter of joy 89
Daughter, the 61
Daughters of Goddess 80
death 41
Death-Goddess 70
Death-Moon 71
debasement 95
debauchery 95
deceiver 89, 95
December 25 .... 70, 75
deception 46
decorations 75
decriminalization of prostitution 80, 83-87
defile 95
degradation 95
degrade 95
deification 63, 93
deification of men 63
deipotent 93
deities 40
Delilah 89
demean 95
Demeter 41
demimondaine 89
Demon est Deus inversus 74
demonization 48
demonization of prostitution 39
demonization, of the Whore-Goddess 70
demonized, sex workers 80

demoralize ... 95
den of iniquity ... 92
den of vice ... 92
Denmark, named after a goddess ... 42
denunciation ... 95
depravity ... 95
depredation ... 95
derision ... 95
desecration ... 95
desertion ... 32, 54
despoil ... 95
detestation ... 95
Devadasis ... 40
devalue ... 72, 95
Devil ... 74, 95
devil worshiper ... 95
Devil, the ... 74
devils of cruelty, sex workers as ... 80
devotion ... 93
Diana ... 3, 120
Dies Natalis Sol Invictus ... 75
dignity ... 93
Dike ... 66
Dionysus ... 56
dirt ... 95
dirty ... 95
disapproval ... 95
disease and prostitution ... 67
disgrace ... 51, 95
disgust ... 95
dishonor ... 95
disrespect ... 63, 95
dissatisfaction, male ... 54
dissipation ... 95
distinction ... 93
diva ... 93
Divine Feminine ... 11, 49, 60, 69, 71, 103, 117, 119
Divine Feminine, among the Jews ... 49
Divine Feminine, and connection to the sea ... 56
Divine Royal Bloodline, of Jesus and Mary Magdalene ... 60
Divine Savior-Son ... 70
Divine Son ... 41, 56-58
Divine Sun/Son-God ... 75
divinity ... 93
divorce ... 32, 38, 54, 67
divorce and prostitution ... 67
divorce rate, in the West ... 54
divorce, women and ... 55
DNA ... 35
dominatrices ... 78
Don Juan ... 89
dove ... 58
doxy ... 89
dragon ... 89
drinking ... 75
drones, men as ... 44

druggie	95
dry-nosed primates	100
dryad	93
Dubhehoblaigh, Queen	167
Dworkin, Andre	38
dykes	66
earliest religions	47
early Hebrews	41
Early Neolithic women	45
Earth	11, 21, 37, 41, 49, 51, 63, 71, 72, 78, 107, 110, 121
Earth-Moon-Mother-Goddess	72
Earth-Mother, worship of	63
Earth-Mother	11, 63
Easter, Pagan	41
Eastern Churches	75
easy make	89
economic considerations	38
Eden	48
educator	93
Edward II	167
Egypt	40, 49, 105, 115, 116, 119, 121, 124
Egyptian Goddess-worship	70
Egyptian religion	65
Egyptians	70
Eighteenth Dynasty, Egyptian	65
Eirene	66
El	49, 62
El Shaddai	11, 64, 65
El, etymology of	65
Elders, Joycelyn	87
elevation	93
Ellis, Havelock	39
Elohim	64
emotional abuse	54
enchantress	89, 95
England	104, 121, 123, 124, 167
English	39, 40, 42, 47, 62, 64, 65, 71-73, 104, 109, 111, 113, 116-119, 123
English language	40, 116
English scribes	47, 64
English sexologist	39
enlightened views	39
enlightener	93
enlightenment	42, 47, 74, 78, 80, 93
Enlil	105
Eostre	41
erect Male Principle, symbol of	52
erect phallus	51
Eriksdottir	76
Eros	56
escort	89, 119
escorts	78
esteem	27, 93
etchings	63
eternal union	61
etymology	40, 57, 61
etymology and the Great Whore-Mother	78

Eunomia 66
Europe . . 3, 40, 42, 56, 57, 60, 63, 70, 73, 74, 78, 103, 107, 108, 111, 113, 118, 120, 121, 123, 168
Europe, named after a goddess 42
Eutheria 100
Eve 48
evil 48, 95
evolution 35
evolutionary background 32
exaltation 93
execration 95
exemplar 93
exploitation 95
extinct humans, list of 78
faith 42, 62, 66, 93
fakery 95
fallen angel 89
fallen woman 89
fame 3, 92, 93
family life, and women 55
family tree of life 100
fancy woman 89
father 2, 11, 17, 33, 40, 46, 48-50, 54, 62-66, 76, 83, 107
father, not part of original nuclear family 33
father, role of unknown 54
Father, Son, and Holy Ghost 57
father-figure 63
father-figure, lack of in early Christian art 33
Father-God 63
Father-God Yahweh, hatred of 50
father-son relationships 46
fatherhood 33, 34, 53
fatherhood, a recent cultural invention 53
Father-God 48-50, 62, 64, 65
father's last name 76
Fatima, Portugal 73
fear 79
feasting 75
Federal Government, U.S. 83
feeding the young 34
felon 95
female   10, 17, 22, 31, 33, 35-37, 42-46, 50-52, 54, 58-61, 63, 65, 67, 69, 71-73, 78-80, 84, 86, 112,
116-118, 121, 167
female breast 65
female breast symbol 65
female infidelity rates 55
Female Principle 45, 61, 65, 69
female prostitutes 69
female prostitutes, prehistoric 35
female prostitution 31, 69
female saints 65
female sex-workers 78
female-exclusive groups 46
female-headed matriarchies 52
female-on-female bond 46
female-on-female friendships 46
female-on-male bond 46

female-on-male friendships ... 46
female-only schools ... 45
female's maternal instincts ... 54
feminine arts ... 45
feminine Deity, in Christianity ... 70
feminine number of fortune ... 73
feminine Pagan calender ... 42
Feminine Power ... 40
Feminine Principle ... 47
feminine psychology ... 113
Feminism ... 111, 121
feminists ... 38, 77
femme fatale ... 95
fertility ... 48
fertility rites ... 48
field ... 117
fille de joie ... 89
filth ... 95
financial support ... 38
fish ... 59, 60
fishwife ... 89
Fitzseward, Sibyl ... 167
floozy ... 89
Flora ... 7
Floralia ... 7
food for sex ... 35
food gathering, early women programmed for ... 33
food sharing ... 36
foraging-and-scavenging groups ... 32
fossil record ... 32, 37
fossil remains ... 63
Founding Fathers ... 83
France ... 59, 60
France, and Jesus' Royal Bloodline ... 59
Frankish kings ... 60
freedom ... 39
freedom-loving polygamous urges ... 55
French royalty, and Jesus' Royal Bloodline ... 59
Freud, Sigmund ... 53
Freya ... 70
friendship, replacing sex with genuine ... 37
Frigg ... 70
Frigga ... 70
Frigga Goddess-worship ... 70
Fury ... 89
Galilee ... 59
Garden of Eden ... 48
gay (male) marriage ... 46
gay marriages ... 46
gene pool ... 35
genes ... 35
Genesis, book of, and Mormon Goddess-worship ... 71
Genesis, creation legend of ... 62
genetic code ... 31
genetic program ... 38
genetically determined behavior ... 31

genetically hard-wired mating strategy 36
genetically programmed prostitution 36
geneticists 35
Gerd 115
German Goddess-worship 73
German high-god 65
Germanic names 71
Germanic words 65
gibbons 100
gift-giving 75
gigolo 89
Gimbutas, Marija A. 63
Ginosko 47, 74, 80
girls 22, 23, 67, 83, 104
global Sisterhood 52
Glooskap 56
Glorious Mother-Goddess 65
glory 93
gnosis 42
Gnosis of the Whore-Goddess 47
Gnostic Christian 13, 59, 116
Gnostic Christian documents 59
Gnostic Christian tradition 59
Gnostic Christianity 13, 59
Gnosticism 60
Gnosticism, original authentic Christianity 41
Gnosticism, original Christianity 74
Gnostics 41, 70, 74
Gnostics, the 41
Gnostics, the (first Christians) 70
Gnosticsim 74
God 42, 61-65, 74
God, etymology of 65
Goda 65
Goddess   3, 7, 9-11, 13, 40-44, 46-52, 56-58, 61-66, 69-80, 89, 93, 103-105, 109-111, 117, 118, 120,
           122, 124, 167, 169
Goddess christing ritual 57
Goddess Dike 66
Goddess Faith 42
Goddess Mother-Moon 72
Goddess names, and the mari element 42
Goddess of Desire 51
Goddess tradition 43
Goddess words 77
Goddess World 44, 46, 69, 76
Goddess World, ancient 46
Goddess-worship, prehistoric 48
Goddess-worship, revival among early Jews 50
Goddess-worshiping Jewish religion 61
Goddess-worshiping matriarchal faith, Judaism as 62
Goddess-worshiping Sisterhood 47
goddesses 23, 41, 48, 56, 70, 71, 103, 106, 111, 116, 117, 119
Goddess' christing oil 57
Goddess' inverted pubic triangle 52
Goddess' lucky numbers 43
Goddess' Lunar Calender 43

Goddess' Old Religion 57
Goddess' priestesses 78
Goddess' sacred bird 58
Goddess' sacred number 51
Goddess' sacred ritual of prostitution 77
Goddess' sacred snake 48
Goddess' Savior-Son 59
Goddess' Temples 43, 52
Goddess-worship 3, 10, 11, 47-50, 61, 70, 120, 169
Goddess-worshipers 50, 72
Goden 65
godhood 71
gods 41, 56, 64, 103-109, 111, 112, 115, 116, 119, 121, 123
Golden Age of Women 44, 63
golden bull heads 60
golden tiara 73
Gorgon 89
gorillas 31, 100
Gospel of Mary, The 58
Gospel of Philip 60
government 83, 85
grace 40, 93
grace of Goddess 40
Graces 41
Grandmother, the 61
Granger, Robert, General 67
great apes 100, 101
great apes, the 101
Great Gnosis 47
Great Mother 43, 51, 78, 118
Great Mother-Goddess 43
Great Triple-Goddess 41
Great Virgin 75
Great Virgin Mother 41
Great Whore of Babylon 70
Great Whore Wisdom 53
Great Whore, modern worship of the 69
Great Whore-Goddess 70
Great Whore-Mother 63
Great Whore-Mother-Goddess 13, 44, 61
greatness 93
Greece 40, 70, 73
Greece, named after a goddess 42
Greek Death-Goddess 70
Greek Father-God 48
Greek God of Healing 48
Greek mythology 41
Greek Sex-Goddess 7, 65
Greek Sun-God 74
Greek word 17
Greek words 47
Greeks 64
ground 41
group marriage 45, 55
Guarantee Clause 83
guards, men as 44

guide	93
Gwair, Afandreg Verch	167
gylanies	52
gylany	17
gylany, defined	17
gynopology	72
hag	89, 105
hallowed	93
hangings, woven	49
Haplorrhini	100
Har	70
Harines	40
Harlot, the	7, 70
harlotry	81, 85, 91
Harlotry, royal profession of	81
harpy	89
harridan	89
harvest	63
harvesting time	49
Hasidic Ashkenazim	49
head, the	42, 58
health and safety, of prostitutes	87
heaven	37, 70, 71, 93, 107
Heavenly Father	64
Heavenly Mother	71
Heavenly Mother, the Mormon	71
heavenly spheres of time	43
heavens	63
hebracization	56, 72
Hebrew Creation myth	48
Hebrew folkdance	49
Hebrew Goddess	50, 118
Hebrew Goddess-worship	50
Hebrew love of Goddess, ancient	49
Hebrew males, early	48
Hebrew matrilineality	62
Hebrew matrilocal marriage	62
Hebrew mythology	48, 64
Hebrew names	48, 72
Hebrew names for God	64
Hebrew priests	48
Hebrew Serpent-God	48
Hebrew Triple-Goddess	48
Hebrew women	62, 70
Hebrew words	47, 57
Hebrew/Jewish priests	64
Hebrews	64
Hebrews, early	48, 65
Hecate	48
Heiros Gamos	43
Hel	71
Hell, etymology of	71
heres	57
heroine	93, 122
Hesus	41, 56, 58
heterosexual marriage	46

heterosexual marriages 46
heterosexual monogamy 40
heterosexual women 46
hexagram 52
hexagramic symbol of Judaism 52
Heylel 74
Hindu Goddess-worship 70, 71, 73
Hindu mythology 40
Hindu temples 40
Hindus 70, 73
hips 50
history of women 78
Hittite 105
Hittites 51
Hivites 51
Hokmah 49
hol 71, 72
hole 40, 71
holiness 93
Holland, named after a goddess 42
holly boughs 75
Holy Blood, Holy Grail (Baigent, Leigh, and Lincoln) 59
holy days 75
Holy Father 62
Holy Ghost 57, 58, 61
Holy Grail 59
Holy Harlots 43
Holy Matrimony 71
Holy Matrimony, meaning of 72
holy mountain 50
Holy Priestesses 40
Holy Trinity 57
Holy Whore 58
Holy Whores 42
holy, etymology of 71
homage 93
home wrecker 95
home wreckers 40
hominid species 78
Hominidae 101
Hominina 101
Homininae 101
Hominini 101
Hominoidea 100
Homo antecessor 78
Homo erectus 31, 78
Homo ergaster 78
Homo floresiensis 78
Homo georgicus 78
Homo habilis 78
Homo heidelbergensis 78
Homo neanderthalensis 78
Homo rudolfensis 78
Homo sapiens 11, 34, 78, 79, 101
Homo sapiens idaltu 78
Homo sapiens sapiens 79, 101

Homo, Genus	78, 101
homophobes	66
homosexual rites	57
hooker	5, 21, 89, 113
hor	40, 49-51, 78
hora	10, 40, 42, 43, 49, 57, 66
Hora, dance	49
Horae	40-43, 66
Horaea	43
Hori	51
Horites	10, 50, 51
horizontal refreshment	91
horologers	77
horology	11, 77
horoscopes	43, 49
Hors	40
Horus	33, 41, 56
hour	40
Houri	40
hours of time	49
house of assignation	92
house of ill fame	92
house of ill pleasure	92
house of ill repute	92
House of Shame	51, 92
House of the Lord, and prostitution	48
house with red doors	92
human babies	33
human brain	32
human culture	53
human cultures	40
human evolution	54
human female	33, 72
human great ape, the	100
human head	58
human mothers	33
human primate	36
human relationships, maternal nucleus of	53
human sisters	36
human society	17, 31, 53, 80
human society, maternal nucleus of	53
humanism	63
humanitarianism	46
humans	100
humans, modern	101
humiliation	95
hunters	44, 54
hunters, men as	44
hunting parties	33
hunting-and-gathering communities	32
Hurrians	51
husband	13, 36, 38
husbands	38, 55, 77
husbands and marital rape	38
hussy	89
hustler	89

Hyacinth 56
Hydra 48
Hylobatidae 100
I AM 64
Iahu, and Yahweh 48
Icenians 167
idolize 93
Ieoud 56
ignorance 39, 57, 79
Illuminati 60
illumination through sex 47
immortality 48
immortalization 93
impudent 50
Inanna 41
incense 75
India 40, 69
Indiana 104, 114, 122, 123
Indo-European languages 74
Indo-European morphemes 78
Indo-European Mother-Goddess 42
Indo-European Triple-Goddess 57
Indo-European word 40
Indo-European world 56, 73
Indo-Europeans 63
Indo-European 40, 42, 56, 57, 73, 74, 78
Indo-European word 40
Indra 56
infants, heads of 32
infants, raising of among lesbians 45
infidelity 32, 54
Innocent IV 66
instructor 93
intellectual knowledge 47
intimate relationships 36
intolerance 79
inverted pubic triangle symbol 52
inverted three-pointed star 41
Ireland 3, 42, 108, 116, 118-120, 167
Ireland, named after a goddess 42
Is-Ra-El 49, 62
Isaac 64
Isabella, Queen 167
Isaiah 41, 49, 61, 62, 74
Isaiah, book of 74
Ishara 48, 49
Ishtar 41, 49, 70
Ishtar-Mari 70
Isis 33, 41, 49, 62, 70, 110, 119, 124
Israel 40, 42, 49, 62
Israel, etymology of 49, 62
Israel, founded by women 62
Israel, Goddess worship in ancient 49
Israel, named after a goddess 42
Israelite Goddess-worship 70
Israelites 10, 47, 49, 57, 70

Israelites, and Goddess-worship 49
Israelites, and Whore Wisdom 47
Israelites, matriarchal 47
Israel's oldest deity 48
Isua 41
Italian 66, 81
Italian madams 66
Italy 42, 66
Italy, named after a goddess 42
Iu-Pater 64
Iu-Pater 64
Iva 56
Jacob 64
jade 89
Jah 61
Jahu 72
Jahveh 72
January 1 42
Jao 56
Japan 108
Japanese Goddess-worship 73
Jason 56, 73
Jefferson, Thomas 19, 83
Jehovah 61, 64, 65, 73
Jeremiah 70
Jerusalem Church 75
Jerusalem Temple 49, 59, 70
Jesus . . . 3, 8, 10, 33, 37, 41, 48, 56, 58-61, 66, 69-71, 73-75, 83, 103, 104, 107, 108, 110, 115, 116,
120, 121, 123, 169
Jesus and Satan, brothers, according to Mormons 71
Jesus and the Gospel of Q (Seabrook) 121
Jesus and the Law of Attraction (Seabrook) 120
Jesus and the royal bloodline 59
Jesus ben Pandira 56
Jesus, as a Sun-God 41
Jesus, as Pagan solar deity 74
Jesus, fish symbol and 60
Jesus' cross 57
Jesus' family tree 59
Jesus' family tree, whores in 59
Jesus' marriage 60
Jesus' royal crown 58
Jesus' three days in womb-cave 58
Jesus' titles 74
Jewish calender 49
Jewish creation legend 62
Jewish Father-God 65
Jewish Goddess-worship 70
Jewish mythographers 61, 73
Jewish polytheism 64
Jewish priests 70
Jewish queens 50
Jewish sects, modern Goddess worship in 49
Jewish temple prostitutes 48, 49
Jewish women, early 59
Jewish worship, of Tammuz 56

Jewish year	41
Jews	41, 47-52, 56, 61, 64, 72, 109
Jews, ancient	47
Jews, and Goddess worship	49
Jews, mystical	52
Jezebel	50, 89
Jezebel's name	50
Joshua	56, 73
Josiah, King	48
Jove	72
joy house	92
Judaism	10, 21, 47, 50-52, 61, 62, 65, 72, 103, 120
Judaism, arose as a Goddess-worshiping religion	62
Judaism, matriarchal	47
Judaism, patriarchal	47
Judeo-Christian God	64
judges, as clients of prostitutes	80
Juno	70
Juno Goddess-worship	70
Jupiter	64, 72
Kabbalism	74
Kabbalists	74
Kadru	48
Kali	70, 71
Kali-Ma	71
Kali-Meri	70
Kansas	124
Kelle	3, 41, 42, 70, 120
Kentucky	168
Kenyanthropus	101
King James	17, 123
King James version	17, 123
King James Version, of Bible	17
King of France	59
Kingdom	3, 8, 80, 100, 120, 121, 169
Kingdom of God	8, 80
KJV	17
knew, sexually	47
know, sexually	47
knowing, sexually	47
knowledge	42
knowledge, intellectual	47
knowledge, Jewish	47
knowledge, spiritual	47
Krishna	56
Kukulcan	56
Kurgans	63
labor	39
Ladies of the Hour	40
Lady Godiva	65, 167
lady of the evening	89
Lamb	42
Lamia	48
language	78
large-brained immature infants	34
Last Supper, The (da Vinci)	60

Late Paleolithic Era 45
Late Paleolithic women 45
laurel 93, 109, 123
law 38
laws, pro-fatherhood 53
LDS 70, 71
Leah 62
legalized prostitution, marriage as 38
legalized rape, marriage as 38
legalizing prostitution, to stop spread of disease 67
lemurs 100
Leo X 66
lesbian colonies 45
lesbian communities 52
lesbian love 45
lesbian marriage 46
lesbian marriages 46
lesbian mating 45
lesbian militia 45
lesbian, origin of word 45
lesbianism 45, 55
lesbians 46, 66
Lesbos 45
lesser apes, the 100
Leviathan 48
Liber Pater 56
licensing sex workers 67
licentious behavior 48
licentious dancing 7
life 41
life force, lacking in men 43
life-giving female energy 42
life-nurturing maternal figure 61
lifelong monogamous marriage 54
lifetime monogamy 32
lifetime monogamy, defined 79
life-giving vulva 50
light o' love 89
Lincoln's War 67
lionization 93
living archaic societies 44
living creatures 62
living in caves 51
living primates 33
Lleu Llaw Gyffes 56
loathsome 95
logical positivism 63
long-haired Frankish kings 60
long-term monogamous relationships 44
long-term monogamy 79
loose flexible relationships 45
loose woman 89
loser 2, 3, 95
loss 95
love 66
love of whores, the 53

Lucifer	74
Ludlow, Daniel H.	71
Lugh	56
lunar crescent	62
lunar crescent, as a symbol of Goddess	62
Lunar Year	41, 49, 72
lunar-solar cult	74
Ma	42
Ma Ma	42, 56
Maachah	50
machines	63
madam	89, 121
Madison, James	83
Madonna	78
maenad	89
Magdalene	89
Magdalene, etymology of	58
magic ceremony	42
Mahavira	56
maiden-name	76
majesty	23, 93
male deity	63
male infidelity rate	54
male polygamy after death, Mormon belief in	71
male power	74
Male Principle	52, 61
male's role in reproduction	44
male's sexual fluid	57
Malta, named after a goddess	42
mammal	78
Mammalia	100
mammals	3, 100
mammary	78
man, etymology of	72
mandatory	98
manifest	52
manifests	36
manipulate	44
manuscript	103
man's embraces	39
Mar	42, 56
mar element	42, 56
Mara	42, 56
March	42
March 21	42
Marduk	56
mare	42
Mari	42, 56, 57, 66, 71, 73, 75
Mari Tare	71, 75
Mari-Anna-Ishtar	41
Maria	42, 56, 78
Mariam	42, 56
Marian	42, 56, 78
Marici	73
Marie	42, 56, 78
marina	42

marinate	42
marine	42
mariner	42
Maris	42, 56, 69
marital rape	38
maritime	42
marriage	53, 67, 68, 75, 77, 78
marriage as legalized prostitution	38
marriage as legalized rape	38
marriage, etymology of	71
marriage, gay (male)	46
marriage, heterosexual	46
marriage, lesbian	46
marriage, none in the Afterlife	37
marriage-as-institutionalized prostitution	77
married men	77
Mars	42
Mary	10, 11, 33, 41, 42, 56, 58-60, 65, 66, 69-71, 73, 78, 106-108, 112, 115, 116, 119, 121
Mary Magdalene	10, 58-60, 65, 66, 112, 115, 116, 119
Mary Magdalene, The Gospel of	58
masculine Christian calender	42
Mass of Christ	75
mate-swapping	45
material	72
material comforts	36
material goods	37
materialism	74
maternal	78
maternal caregivers, women as	54
maternal energy	65
maternal figure	53
maternal instincts	54
maternal symbolism	50
maternal warmth	46
math	78
matri	72
matriarch	10, 17, 47, 51, 61-63, 78, 80, 105, 167
matriarchal	10, 17, 47, 61-63, 80, 105, 167
matriarchal Europe	63
matriarchal Goddess-worshiping religion	61
matriarchal marriage, defined	17
matriarchal religions	47
Matriarchate	10, 51
Matriarchate, the	61
Matriarchies	33, 63
matriarchies, ancient	46
matricentric	3, 120
matrifocal	51, 63
matrifocal belief-system	63
matrilocal	62
matrimony	54, 78
matrimony, etymology of	72
matrix	78
Matron	7
matronymicism	17, 76
Matrum Noctem	75

matter 72, 78
May 13 73
May Day 7
Maya 42, 56
Mead, Margaret 53
medical role, of sex workers 80
medicine, symbol of 48
Medieval Catholicism 81
Medieval Christian mythographers 65
Medieval English scribes 47, 64
Mediterranean Sea 59
Medusa 48, 89
memory 78
men 35, 38, 43-45, 54, 63, 69, 76, 78, 80
men as providers of material support 36
men, killing and maiming of 45
menarche 78
menhir 78
menopause 78
menorah 78
menses 78
menstrual 78
menstrual blood 42
menstrual cycle 43
menstruation 78
mental abuse 54
mentor 93, 112
merciful 94
mercy 14, 80, 93
mere 42
Meretri 7
meri 41, 42, 56
mermaid 42, 78
Merovech the Young, King 60
Merovee 60
Merovingian tombs 60
Merovingians 60
Mesoamerican Paganism, and Mormonism 71
Mesopotamian words 73
mess up 96
metallurgy 78
metamorphosis 78
Metazoa 100
meteor 78
meteorology 78
Meter 78
metestrus 78
metric 78
metrology 78
metronymy 17
metronymy, defined 17
Middle Ages 66
middle ear bones 100
Middle East 115, 121
Mikado 56
milk of human kindness 65

milk production 100
milk-giving breast 65
mind 78
mind of Christ, the 74
Minerva 73
miniature golden bees 60
Minne 66
Miriam 41, 42, 56
misogynistic attitudes 79
misogynistic Jewish priests 51
misogynistic mythology 39
misogyny 52
missionary position, introduction of 52
mistletoe 75
mistranslated 64
mistranslation 57
mistress 89, 94
Mithra 56
Mithras 56
Mitra 56
modern age 45
modern humans 37, 101
modern prostitute 39
Moerae, the 42, 56
molestation 96
moll 90
mom 78
mon 72
mon element 71
monarch 78
monarchy 78
monastery 78
Monday 72, 78
Monday, etymology of 72
monetary 78
money 39, 78, 80
monkeys 100
monogamous bond 38
monogamous marriage 31, 38, 54, 67, 77, 79
monogamous marriage, in ancient Rome 54
monogamous romantic relationship 46
monogamy 78
monogamy as a sin 44
monogamy, lifelong 54
monogamy, prohibition of 44
monogamy, women's rejection of 44
monolith 78
monotheism 65
mons veneris 51, 78
month 41, 42, 49, 72, 73, 78
Moon 3, 41, 43, 49, 58, 61, 62, 71-73, 75, 78, 103, 112, 120
Moon, Dark 58
Moon, New 58
Moon, Old 58
Moon-based Jewish calender 49
Moon-Goddess 75

Moon-Mother-Goddess Creation myth 41
Moon's Day 72
moor 78
mor element 71
morganatic 78
morje 42
Mormo 71
Mormo, goddess who gave her name to the Mormons 71
Mormon belief, that Jesus and Satan are brothers 71, 74
Mormon, word related to ancient female words 78
Mormonism 74
Mormonism, and Goddess-worship 70, 71
Mormons 70, 71
Mormons, as followers of Mormo 71
Mormons, Quetzalcoatl, and Jesus 48
morning 78
Morning Star 70, 74
Morrigan 48
mortuary 78
Moses 48, 64
mother 3, 9-11, 13, 17, 33, 37, 40-46, 49, 51-53, 56-58, 61-63, 65, 70-73, 75, 78, 94, 104, 110,
113, 118, 120, 121
mother and child, as the true nuclear family 33
Mother Archetype 56
Mother in Heaven 71
Mother in Heaven, the Mormon 71
Mother of Harlots 70
Mother, the 61
mother-daughter relationships 46
Mother-Earth 41
Mother-Goddess 43, 49, 58, 62
Mother-Goddess, the Mormon 71
Mother-Goddess, worship of among Christians 70
Mother-Harlot 51
Mother-Nature 45
Mother-Whore-Goddess 73
motherhood 97
mothering 94
motherly love 53
mothers 33
Mothers and Bachelors (Seabrook) 37
mound 78
Mound of Venus 51
Mount Hor 50
mountain 50, 65, 78
mountain, holy 50
mountain-goddess 65
mountains 42
mountains, named after goddesses 42
mouth 60
Mu 42, 56
multi-orgasmic response, women's 44
multiple husbands 45
multiple wives 77
multistoried buildings, and the thirteenth floor 58
muse 78

Mu'Allidtu 51
Mylitta 51
Mylitta's female followers 51
myrrh 78
Myrrha 41, 42, 56
mystical feminine tradition 59
mystical Jews 52
mystical symbolism 58
mystics 42, 53, 74
mystics, and Whore Wisdom 53
myth 2, 9, 40, 41, 48, 62, 83-87, 103-113, 115, 120, 122
mythographers 61, 65, 71, 73
mythology 39-41, 48, 56, 59, 64, 104, 106, 107, 109-116, 118-124
myths 12, 40, 72, 83, 104-109, 111, 112, 114, 118, 121, 123, 124
myths, early 40
nag 90, 113, 119
naiad 94
Nashville, Tennessee 5, 27, 67
Nature 37
Nature as sexist 37
Neanderthal 79
Near East 105, 123
Near-Eastern serpent cults, early 48
Near-Eastern Whore-Goddess 66
Nehustan 48
neocortex 100
Neolithic 40, 44, 45, 62, 76, 113
Neolithic Creation Myth 62
Neolithic Era 40, 44
Neolithic settlements 76
Nessa 124
Nevada 121
New Lunar Year 41
New Moon 58
New Testament 47, 58, 73, 74
New Year, the original Pagan 42
New Zealand, prostitution decriminalized in 87
Night of the Mother 75
Ninhursag 41
Nirvana 80, 94
nixie 90
noble heritage 78
nomadic bachelorhood groups 35
non-Bible based "Christian" churches 70
nonhuman apes 32
nonhuman female primates 46
nonhuman great apes 100
nonhuman primates 36, 37, 53
North America 3
North Carolina 168
Northern European Goddess-worship 70
Norwegian Goddess-worship 73
nuclear family 33
nuclear family, the true 33
nunneries 66
nuns 81

nurse 94
nurses, sex workers as 80
nursing mother 61, 65
nurturer 94
nurturing 50, 61, 65, 94
nymph 94
nymphomaniac 90
objective studies 37
occult mysteries 60
occult symbols 52
ocean 42, 53, 59
oceanic amniotic fluid 62
Odin 41, 56
offering sex 35
offspring 35
ogress 90
oil, sacred 42
Oklahoma 123
Old English 42, 72
Old Moon 58
Old Religion 41, 48, 57
Old Testament 11, 47, 50, 61, 74, 107, 110, 112
oldest profession 31, 77
Omikami Amaterasu 73
omnipotent 94
on the game 91, 108
One, the 25
orangutans 31, 100
orgasm 43
orgies 7
Oriental Jews 49
Original Sin 119
origins of prostitution 34
Orontes 56
Orrorin 101
orthodox Christian priests 75
orthodox Christianity, arrival of 52
Osiris 56, 105
out-of-wedlock births 32
outrage 96
Pagan aspects of Jesus 59
Pagan Crone-Goddess 57
Pagan Father-God 49
Pagan Goddess 49
Pagan Goddesses 71
Pagan Greek Savior-God-King 56
Pagan Holy Whores 66
Pagan religions 64
Pagan Rome 75
Pagan Sacrificial Savior-Son-God 49
Pagan Savior 73
Pagan Savior-Son-God 57
Pagan Savior-Sun-God 41
Pagan Saviors 56
Pagan Semitic phrase-word 64
Pagan Snake-God, and Mormons 48

Pagan Spring Festival	41
Pagan Sun-God	65, 72
Paganism	107, 124
Paganism of Christmas	75
paganization of Jesus	74, 75
paid sex worker	38
painted woman	90
paintings	63
paintings, ancient	45
pair-bonding	31
pair-bonds	31
Paleolithic	45
Pales	49
Palestine	49
Palestine, Goddess-worship in	51
Palestine, named after a goddess	42
Pan	56
Pan paniscus	36
pander	91
pandering	91
pansexuality	31
Papa	108
paramour	90
Paranthropus	101
parental care	33
parenting	34
Parilia	49
parthenogenesis	44, 70
passage of the seasons	42
paternal figure	53
paternal love	53
paternity	44, 53
patriarchal culture	50
patriarchal Hebrew priests	48, 50
patriarchal hierarchy, Judaic	47
patriarchal Jewish priests	51
patriarchal Judaism	47
patriarchal Judeo-Christian-based society	77
patriarchal marriage	17
patriarchal marriage, defined	17
patriarchal men	69
patriarchal misogynists	74
patriarchal phobias	79
patriarchal priests	51
patriarchal symbolism	75
Patriarchal Takeover	10, 11, 45, 47, 56, 63, 72
patriarchal warriors	63
patriarchalists	60, 63, 72
patriarchies	33
patricization	51
patricized	51
patrifocal belief-system	63
patrons of prostitutes	65
patronymicism	17, 76
patronymy, defined	17
peaceful mode of living	46

Pennsylvania 114
Pentheus 56
perception of Yada 47
Peris 41
Persia 40
Persian mythology 41
personal rights 39
personifications of Goddess 61
perversion 96
pervert 79, 90, 96
phallic rockets 63
phallus signs 51
phallus, anointing the 42
phallus, head of 58
Phanes 118
Pharaoh 65
Pheterson, Gail 25, 97
Phoebus 74
Phoenicia 51, 70
Phoenician Goddess-worship 70
phone sex operators 78
physical abuse 54
physical pleasure 36
pickup 90
piece of tail 90
piercing 41
pine trees 75
pit 40
pity 96
placenta 100
planets 71
Platonic love 37
Platonic relationships 46
plurality of deities, Mormon belief in a 71
Plutarch 65
Pluto 108
poetry 45
police officers, as clients of prostitutes 39, 80
political correctness 37
politically correct vocabulary 38
politically incorrectness 37
politicians, as clients of prostitutes 80
politics 17, 78, 108, 112, 117, 168
pollutants 63
pollution 96
polyamory 55
polyandry 45, 55
polygamous societies, and prostitution 67
polygamy 32, 45
polygamy, serial 55
polygyny 77
polytheism 64
Pongidae 100
pool 42
Pope Gregory XIII 42
popes 66

popularity 38, 69, 94
Porne 7, 70
pornography, etymology of word 70
praise 94
prayers 75
pre-Christian Pagan Mother-Whore-Goddess 73
pre-Christian saviors 59
pre-Christian Syrian Pagan Savior 73
pre-Judaic Indo-European word 40
pre-scientific period 44
preceptor 94
predators 112
pregnant abdomen 50
prehistoric ancestors 31, 37, 67
prehistoric females 34
prehistoric Goddess-worship 48
prehistoric men 31
prehistoric origins, of prostitution 31-34
prehistoric peoples 63, 79
prehistoric women 31
prestige 39, 94
prestige, power, and privilege 39
priestess 9, 40, 90, 94
priestesses 40, 42, 44, 78
priests 48-51, 62, 64, 75
primal custom 32
primate ancestors 78
primate babies 33
primate heritage 46
primate males 33
primate mothers 33
primate species 36
Primates, order of 100
primatological dictates 45
primatologists 33, 36
primitive symbols 63
Princess Diana: Modern Day Moon-Goddess (Seabrook) 120
Priory of Scion 60
pro-family 18
pro-fidelity 18
pro-marriage 18
pro-monogamy 18
procreative life-force 58
procreative powers 41
procreative process, men and 44
procuress 90
profane 96, 109
Prohibition 84
Prometheus 56
promiscuity 31
promiscuous 18, 31, 96
prostitute .. 10, 12, 22, 36, 38-40, 42, 48, 50, 53, 60, 80, 84, 89, 93, 95, 98, 99, 104, 110, 116, 119, 122
prostitute as paid sex worker 38
prostitute-maternal archetype 53
prostitute-priestesses 40

prostitutes .. 7-9, 35, 39, 40, 48, 49, 51, 54, 59, 65-67, 69, 70, 74, 79-81, 83, 84, 86, 87, 97-99, 123
prostitutes, and popes 66
prostitutes, marrying 48
prostitutes, Roman 51
prostitution .. 3, 5-7, 9-12, 17-19, 21, 22, 27, 31-40, 47, 48, 51, 61, 66, 67, 69, 75, 77-80, 83-87, 91, 92, 97-99, 103, 106, 108, 112-114, 118-121, 123
prostitution gene 35, 36, 79
prostitution gene, defined 35
prostitution, and divorce rates 67
prostitution, approved by Augustine 18, 22, 66, 67, 85
prostitution, involuntary 85
prostitution, voluntary 85
prostitution-based sexual behavior 32
prostitutionary partnerships 38
prostitutionary relationship 36
prostitutionary relationships 39, 67, 79
protecting the young 34
protection for sex 35
Protector of Prostitutes 7
Protestant Churches 75
Psalms, book of 61
pseudo-Christian faiths 70
psychic nucleus 53
psychologists 53
pubic triangle 41
pubic triangle symbol 52
pure 94
Puritans 75
purity 94
putain 90
pyramid 123
qadeshah 49
Quakers, and Goddess-worship 70
Queen of Heaven 70
queens, Jewish 50
Quetzalcoatl 48, 56, 71
Quinotaur 59
Ra 49, 62
Rachab 8, 59
rachaph 62
Rachel 62
radical feminists 22, 33, 38, 54, 85
rain 9, 32, 54, 63, 79, 100
rational materialism 63
Ravensdale, Cassidy 25
Rebirth of the Invincible Sun-God 75
recognition 94
red erect phallus signs 51
red-light district 51, 92
redemption 94
regal tradition 79
religion ... 17, 21, 27, 40, 41, 46-48, 51, 52, 57, 61, 63, 65, 69, 74, 78, 94, 104, 105, 107, 109, 110, 113, 115, 118, 120-123, 168
religions 27, 47, 48, 53, 64, 103, 105, 107-109, 111-113, 122, 124
religious prejudice 79
religious teacher 94

remarriage ... 32
renown ... 94
repute ... 92, 94
respect ... 27, 94
resurrection ... 41, 59, 75, 105
Revelation ... 41, 51, 70, 73, 74
revere ... 94
reverence ... 94
reverent ... 94
revile ... 96
revitalize the soil ... 41
risen Savior ... 59
ritual sacrifice ... 45
rivers, named after goddesses ... 42
Roman Cattle-Goddess ... 49
Roman Christians ... 74
Roman Goddess-worship ... 70, 73
Roman mythology ... 41
Roman Spring-Goddess ... 7
Roman tomb ... 74
romance ... 32, 37
Romania, named after a goddess ... 42
Romans, the ... 51, 54, 64, 73, 75
Rome, ancient ... 49, 51, 74, 75
Rome, Italy ... 66
root-words ... 78
royal blood ... 59
ruination ... 96
Russia ... 63
Ruth ... 8, 59
Sabazius ... 56
sacred female energy ... 58
Sacred Grove of Goddess ... 49
sacred oil ... 42, 58
sacred prostitute ... 50, 119, 122
sacred prostitution ... 7, 40, 69, 75
sacred prostitution and Judaism ... 47
sacred prostitution, among the Jews ... 48
Sacred Sacrificial Lamb ... 42
sacred serpent ... 48
sacred sex with strangers ... 51
sacred sign ... 41
sacred tree groves ... 50
Sacred Union ... 43
Sacred Whore Wisdom ... 78
Sacred Whoredom ... 81
sacred whores ... 40, 44
sacrificial death ... 70
sacrilege ... 96
sacrosanct ... 94
safety ... 19, 85, 87
sage ... 94
Sahelanthropus ... 101
Saint Agape ... 66
Saint Anne ... 57
Saint Aphrodite ... 65

Saint Augustine 18, 22, 66, 85
Saint Charity 66
Saint Chionia 66
Saint Faith 66
Saint Hope 66
Saint Irene 66
Saint Maudline 65
Saint Paul 18, 52, 57, 71, 74
Saint Peter 74
Saint Peter's Basilica 74
Saint Sarah 59
Saint Sophia 66
saintly 94
saints 65
Sakia 56
Samadhi 80
san gréal 59
sanctified 94
sanctity 94
sang réal 59
Saoshyant 56
sapiens, species 101
Sappho 45
Sarah, daughter of Jesus and Mary Magdalene 59
Satan 71, 74, 96
satanic 96
Saturn 75
Saturnalia 75
Savior 33, 41, 49, 56, 57, 59, 70, 73
Savior and Redeemer 41
Savior-Son 70
Savior-Sun/Son 41
Saviors, list of pre-Christian 56
Savior-Son-God 49, 57
scab 39
Scandinavia 42, 70, 76, 108, 109
Scandinavia, named after a goddess 42
Scandinavian Goddess-worship 70
scholars 83, 117
schooling men in sexual mysteries 42
science 63, 77, 168
scorn 96
Scotland 42, 111, 122, 124, 167
Scotland, named after a goddess 42
screw up 96
sea 42
Seabrook, Lochlainn 21, 22, 27, 120, 167
Seabrook's Bible Dictionary (Seabrook) 121
seasons 15, 42, 49
secret knowledge, of Jesus 60
secret marriage, of Jesus and Mary Magdalene 59
secular commercial prostitution 69
secular prostitution 69
seducer 90
seductress 96
seeds, planting of 49

self-fertilizing 44
self-godhood, Mormon belief in 71
semen 57
Semitic culture 50
Semitic peoples 47
Semitic version of Zeus 48
Semitic Whore-Goddess 48
Semitic word 40
Semitic words 65, 71
separate living quarters 62
Sephardim 49
seraphic 94
serial monogamy 32
serial polygamy 32, 45, 55, 79
serpent 48, 90
serpent, Genesaic 48
Serpent-God 48
serpent-goddesses 48
servants, men as 44
seven-day week 72
sex 35-37, 42, 80
sex act, and enlightenment 47
sex care providing business 23
sex objects 36
sex rites 48
sex symbol 94
sex work industry 69, 80
sex worker 39
sex worker, wife as 38
sex workers 67, 69, 78-80
sex workers, individual 80
sex, none in the Afterlife 37
sex, uncomplicated 84
Sex- and Love-Goddess 80
Sex-Goddess 51
sexism 37
sexologists 77
sexpot 96
sexual act 45
sexual activities 31
sexual behavioral pattern 31
sexual companions 44
sexual companions, men as 44
sexual contract 38
sexual dimorphism 33
sexual intercourse 86
sexual mysteries 42
sexual obligations 38
sexual oil 57
sexual position, preferred by women 45
sexual services 38
sexual services for material support 38
sexual services, wives and 77
sexually receptive females 36
sexually submissive roles 52
sexy females 35

shack job ... 90
shaddai ... 11, 64, 65
Shaddai, etymology of ... 65
Shakers ... 70
Shakers, the, and Goddess-worship ... 70
Shakti ... 40, 43, 58
shame ... 13, 50, 92, 96
shameless ... 50
Shaw, George Bernard ... 38
Shekhina ... 49
shemen ... 57
Shemesh ... 56
shining ... 73
short-term monogamy ... 79
short-term pair-bonding ... 32
shrew ... 90
shrines ... 51
shrines, Goddess ... 51
sick ... 96
sickness ... 96
Simiiformes ... 100
sin ... 96
sin of monogamy ... 44
single-gender schools, superior to coed schools ... 33
singular high-god ... 65
sinner ... 96
sins ... 41
siren ... 90
sister ... 94
Sisterhood, the great ... 46, 52
sisterhoods, all-female ... 33
sisters ... 46
Sixtus IV ... 66
sky ... 11, 63
Sky-Father ... 64
Sky-Father, worship of ... 63
slattern ... 90
sleep around ... 91
sloven ... 90
slut ... 90, 96
sluts ... 36
slutty ... 96
small-brained mature infants ... 34
snake ... 48, 90
Snake Cult, Hebrew ... 48
snake worship ... 48
Snake-God, and Mormons ... 48
snakes ... 48
social safety valve, prostitution as ... 67, 85
socialization ... 54
socializing men, for family life ... 54
society ... 40, 46, 47, 53, 61, 77, 80, 81
sodomite ... 96
sodomites ... 51
sodomy ... 96
Sol ... 73

soldiers 68
soldiers and sex workers 67
Solomon, King 50
Solomon's Seal 52
Son 74, 75
Son of God 74
Son of Man 56
Son of Righteousness 56
Son-God 57
Son-Gods, list of pre-Christian 56
song 45
Sonne 74
Sons of God 80
Sophia 49, 66
sorceress 90
soul love 37
soul, the 53
Spender, Dale 38
Sphinx 48
Spirit 3, 42, 94, 110, 123
spiritual enlightenment 42
spiritual enlightenment through sex 78, 80
spiritual knowledge 47
spiritual marriage 37
spiritual role, of sex workers 80
spirituality 74, 94
spiritually enlightened 60
Spring Equinox 42, 70
spring planting 41
sprite 94
squander 96
St. James, Margo 25
staff, winged 48
star 41, 52, 73, 94
Star of the Sea 42, 56, 69, 70
statuettes 63
STDs, rates of 84
Stella Maris 42, 56, 69
stigma 96-99
stone etchings 45
Stossel, John 18
street-walkers 78
streetwalker 90
strumpet 90
stupidity 96
sugar daddies 36, 66
Sulis 73
Sun 11, 41, 57, 63, 65, 72-75, 110, 111
Sun of Righteousness 74
Sun of Righteousness, Jesus as the 41
Sun, as male 63
Sun-God 41, 57, 65, 72, 75
Sun-God of On 50
Sun-God, Jesus as the Christian 41
Sun-Goddess 73, 75
Sun/Son-God 57

Sun/Son-God, death of	41
Sunday	72
Sunday, etymology of	72
Sunna	73
Sun-God	11, 41, 57, 65, 72, 74, 75
Sun's Day	72
superior intellectual powers, of women	44
superior sexual powers, of women	44
Supreme Being	52, 61-63, 70, 71, 79
Supreme Being, female	71
Supreme God	65
survival mechanism, prostitution as a	35
sweat glands	100
swollen life-giving vulva	50
sylph	94
symbiosis between marriage and prostitution	67
symbol of Goddess	41
symbol of Jesus, fish	60
symbol of modern medicine	48
Syrian Savior	59
tainted	96
Tammuz	41, 56, 59, 70
Tantric Buddhist Goddess-worship	73
Tantric mysteries	70
Tantric Path	80
tart	90
taxonomic classification, of human beings	100
teacher	74, 94
teaching of Yada	47
temple	10, 42, 43, 47-51, 58, 59, 70, 78
temple life at Jerusalem	47
temple priestesses	43
temple prostitutes	48, 70
Temple Whores	59
temple-priestesses	42
temples of the whores	51
temporary monogamous relationships	32
temporary pair-bond	32
temptress	90, 96
tenderness	46
Tennessee	3, 5, 6, 27, 67, 168
Tenth Amendment	83
Tetrapoda	100
Teutonic word form	65
Texas	107
Thamar	8, 59
The Bible and the Law of Attraction (Seabrook)	120
The Book of Kelle (Seabrook)	42, 70, 120
The Complete Dictionary of Christian Mythology (Seabrook)	121
The Concise Book of Owls (Seabrook)	121
The Concise Book of Tigers (Seabrook)	121
The Gospel of Mary	58
the Law	3, 38, 103, 120, 169
The National Review	22, 87
The One	14, 15, 25, 42, 62
the Son	41, 60, 74

The Thunder: Perfect Mind ... 13
thealogy ... 27
theists ... 80
theologians ... 83
theology ... 114
Theria ... 100
Third Eye ... 74
thirteen ... 10, 43, 49, 51, 58, 72, 73
thirteen, magic number ... 73
thirteen, magic number of Virgin Mary ... 73
thirteen, sacred Goddess number demonized ... 51
thirteen-month Lunar calender ... 49
thirteen-month Lunar Year ... 72
thirteenth day, Virgin Mary visitations ... 73
thirteenth floor ... 58
thirteen-month Lunar Year ... 72
Thor ... 56
three Marys ... 57
three-pointed star ... 41
Thules ... 56
thunder ... 63
Thuringians, the ... 59
Tiamat ... 48
Tiberius, Octavia Major ... 167
time ... 42
time-keepers ... 77
traditional polygamy ... 32
trainer ... 94
tramp ... 90
tramps ... 36
transfer of procreative power ... 43
trash ... 96
tree, as crucifix ... 57
trees ... 75
triangle ... 41
tribal clan mother ... 44
tribute ... 2, 3, 94, 121
Triple-Goddess ... 41, 48, 57
triplicate-symbolism ... 41
trollop ... 90
trollops ... 36
Troubadours, the ... 66
true nuclear family ... 33
trull ... 90
tutor ... 94
twelve ... 43, 44, 58, 64, 73, 118
Twelve Apostles ... 58
twelve astrological male gods ... 64
Twelve Disciples ... 58
Twelve Holy Harlots ... 58
twelve priestesses ... 44
twelve star-children ... 73
twelve stars ... 73
Twelve Temple Harlots ... 58
Twelve Titans ... 64
twelve-star tiara ... 73

twenty-eight day Lunar phases 43
twenty-eight day Lunar Year 49
twenty-eight day menstrual cycle 43
twenty-eight day months 43
twenty-eight day Moon cycle 72
two-parent family 33, 54
two-parent family, lacking in early humans 33
U.S. army, legalizes prostitution 67, 68
U.S. Constitution 83
ugliness 96
ugly 80, 96
UK 32
understanding of Yada 47
underworld 70, 71
Underworld-Goddesses 71
unearthly 94
union of Female and Male Principles 52
union wages 39
Unitarians, and Goddess-worship 70
Universe 62, 64
unnatural form of bonding 44
unpaid sex worker 38
untapped work force 35
upward pointing triangle 52
Urias 59
USA 32, 69
utilitarian roles, men and 44
vagabond males 35
vagabond-hunter programming, in men 54
vagabonds 33
vagina 86
Valerius Maximus 65
Valla, Lorenzo 81
vamp 96
vegetation 63
veneration 63, 94
venereal disease 67
venery 91
Ventura, Jesse 18
Venus 41, 51, 74
verbal abuse 54
vernal equinox 41
Vertebrata 100
vice 2, 92, 96
victory 94
village 110
violate 19, 96
violence 46, 83, 97
virago 90
virgin birth 70
Virgin Mary 33, 41, 42, 56, 69-71, 73
virgin mother, origin of the idea of the 44
Virgin Mothers 44
Virgin Whore-Mother 56
Virgin, the 75
Virgin-Goddess 58

Virgin-Mother-Goddess	41
Virgin-Whore-Mother-Goddess	49, 75
Virginia	114, 117, 168
virginity	81
Virgo	75
vitiation	96
vixen	90
void	58
vulva	10, 50, 51, 58, 63
vulva of Goddess	51
vulva-worshipers	51
vulvaic triangle	63
V-girl	90
wandering lifestyle	35
wanton	90
War for Southern Independence	67
War to Prevent Southern Independence	67
warrioresses	45
warriors, men as	44
Washington	6
waste	96
watcher of the hours	43
water	42, 62
Way, the	80
Webster, Daniel	77
Wednesday	65
wench	90, 96
wenching	91
Western countries, divorce rate in	54
Western society, and patriarchal marriage	17
Whore	7, 40, 42, 50, 78
Whore of Babylon, the	51
Whore Wisdom	13, 42, 47, 53, 58, 61, 78
Whore Wisdom, in early Judaism	48
whore, etymology of	40
whore-bride	60
Whore-Goddess	41, 47, 62, 65, 66, 69, 73, 74
Whore-Madonna Complex	53
Whore-Mother	65, 73, 75, 78
Whore-Mother religion	51
Whore-Mother-Goddess	44, 65, 73, 78
Whore-Mother-Goddess, and Mormonism	71
Whore-Mother-Goddess' temples	52
Whore-Skopus	43
Whore-Wisdom-Goddess	66
whorehouse	11, 51, 66, 92
whorehouses	66
whores	36, 39, 40, 81
whores, vital roles of	40
Whore-Goddess	10, 11, 41, 42, 47-49, 56, 62, 64-66, 69, 70, 73-75
whore's trade	77
whoring	91
whorish females	35
wide flaring hips	33
wife	39
wife as prostitute	36, 38

wife as unpaid sex worker 38
wife of God, Goddess as 71
wife of Yahweh 62
William I the Conqueror 167
winter solstice 75
wisdom 48, 66
witch 50, 90, 96
witches, the murder of 51
Witoba 56
wives 38, 77
Woden 56, 65
Woden's Day 65
woman 78
Woman deified 63
woman of the streets 90
woman-exclusive cities 45
woman-exclusive villages 45
womb of Goddess 62
womb-cave 58
women .. 15, 18, 21, 22, 31, 35, 36, 38, 44-46, 51-55, 58, 59, 62, 63, 68, 69, 72, 75, 76, 78, 80, 81,
                                                                          83, 85, 86, 98
women and early lesbianism 45
women as providers of sex 36
Women in Gray (Seabrook) 121
women-hating Jewish priests 62
women-only island villages 52
Women's Movement 38
Women's Spirituality Movement 3, 120
Word, the 49
working girl 90
World Egg 48
World Serpent 48
worldwide family 53
worship 47-51, 63, 66, 72, 73, 75, 78, 94, 95
wretched sinners 40
writing 78
writing of harlots 70
Yada 47, 74
Yahi 72
Yahoweh 73
Yahweh 48, 61, 64, 65, 72
Yahweh, hatred of 50
Yahweh, wife of 62
Yhwh 72
Yoni 51, 71, 72
Yoni-worship 51
Yule logs 75
Zagreus 56
Zalmoxis 56
Zeus 48, 64, 72
Zion 49
Zodiac 49
zodiacal circle dances 49
Zoroastra 56

THE AUTHOR'S GENEALOGY

MATRIARCHAL CONNECTIONS

A professional genealogist who has helped many people find their ancestors, Lochlainn Seabrook continues the lifelong research of his own family history.

Descending from a long line of powerful women and Goddess-worshipers, some of Seabrook's more notable female ancestors include: Queen Boudicca of the ancient Icenians (Seabrook's 40th great-grandmother), Queen Sibyl Fitzseward of Scotland (his 27th great-grandmother), Queen Dubhehoblaigh of Ireland (34th great-grandmother), Afandreg Verch Gwair Princess of Wales (30th great-grandmother), Saint Margaret Atheling Queen of Scotland and England (26th great-grandmother), "Lady Godiva" Countess of Mercia (31st great-grandmother), Queen Matilda Baldwin of England (26th great-grandmother and the wife of William I the Conqueror), Queen Isabella "the Fair" of England (23rd great-grandmother and the wife of Edward II King of England), Queen Thyra Danebod of Denmark (32nd great-grandmother), and Empress Octavia Major Tiberius of Rome (43rd great-grandmother and the wife of Mark Anthony Emperor of Rome).

MEET THE AUTHOR

Neo-Victorian scholar Lochlainn Seabrook, a descendant of the families of Alexander Hamilton Stephens, John Singleton Mosby, Edmund Winchester Rucker, and William Giles Harding, is a 7th generation Kentuckian and the most prolific and popular pro-South writer in the world today. Known by literary critics as the "new Shelby Foote" and by his fans as the "Voice of the Traditional South," he is a recipient of the prestigious Jefferson Davis Historical Gold Medal, and, as a lifelong writer, has authored and edited books ranging in topics from history, politics, and science, to nature, religion, and the paranormal.

One of the world's most popular living historians, he is a 17th generation Southerner of Appalachian heritage who descends from dozens of patriotic Revolutionary War soldiers and Confederate soldiers from Kentucky, Tennessee, North Carolina, and Virginia. A proud member of the Sons of the Confederate Veterans, he is a true Renaissance Man. Besides being an accomplished and well respected author-historian and Bible authority, he is also a Kentucky Colonel, eagle scout, screenwriter, nature, wildlife, and landscape photographer, artist, graphic designer, songwriter, film composer, musician, music producer, genealogist, former history museum docent, and a former ranch hand, zookeeper, and wrangler.

His 70 adult and children's books contain some 60,000 well-researched pages that have earned him accolades from around the globe. His works, which have sold on every continent except Antarctica, have introduced hundreds of thousands to vital facts that have been left out of our mainstream books. He has been endorsed internationally by leading experts, museum curators, award-winning historians, bestselling authors, celebrities, filmmakers, noted scientists, well regarded educators, TV show hosts and producers, renowned military artists, esteemed heritage organizations, and distinguished academicians of all races, creeds, and colors. Colonel Seabrook also holds the world record for writing the most books on Southern icon Nathan Bedford Forrest: 12.

Of northern and central European descent, he is the 6th great-grandson of the Earl of Oxford and a descendant of European royalty. His modern day cousins include: Johnny Cash, Elvis Presley, Lisa Marie Presley, Billy Ray and Miley Cyrus, Patty Loveless, Tim McGraw, Lee Ann Womack, Dolly Parton, Pat Boone, Naomi, Wynonna, and Ashley Judd, Ricky Skaggs, the Sunshine Sisters, Martha Carson, Chet Atkins, Patrick J. Buchanan, Cindy Crawford, Bertram Thomas Combs (Kentucky's 50th governor), Edith Bolling (second wife of President Woodrow Wilson), Andy Griffith, Riley Keough, George C. Scott, Robert Duvall, Reese Witherspoon, Lee Marvin, Rebecca Gayheart, and Tom Cruise.

A constitutionalist and avid gun advocate, Colonel Seabrook is the author of the international blockbuster, *Everything You Were Taught About the Civil War is Wrong, Ask a Southerner!* He lives with his wife and family in beautiful historic Middle Tennessee, the heart of the Confederacy.

For more information on the author visit
LochlainnSeabrook.com

LOCHLAINN SEABROOK ~ 169

If you enjoyed this book you will be interested in Mr. Seabrook's related popular titles:

- JESUS & THE LAW OF ATTRACTION: THE BIBLE-BASED GUIDE TO CREATING PERFECT HEALTH, WEALTH, & HAPPINESS
- JESUS & THE GOSPEL OF Q: CHRIST'S PRE-CHRISTIAN TEACHINGS AS RECORDED IN THE NEW TESTAMENT
- SEABROOK'S BIBLE DICTIONARY OF TRADITIONAL AND MYSTICAL CHRISTIAN DOCTRINES
- CHRISTMAS BEFORE CHRISTIANITY: HOW THE BIRTHDAY OF THE "SUN" BECAME THE BIRTHDAY OF THE "SON"
- CHRIST IS ALL & IN ALL: REDISCOVERING YOUR DIVINE NATURE & THE KINGDOM WITHIN
- BRITANNIA RULES: GODDESS-WORSHIP IN ANCIENT ANGLO-CELTIC SOCIETY

Available from Sea Raven Press and wherever fine books are sold

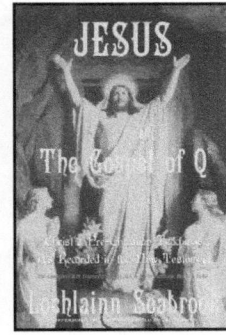

ALL OF OUR BOOK COVERS ARE AVAILABLE AS 11" X 17" POSTERS, SUITABLE FOR FRAMING.

SeaRavenPress.com

www.ingramcontent.com/pod-product-compliance
Lightning Source LLC
Chambersburg PA
CBHW032054090426
42744CB00005B/214